Vampire

De Havilland's First Generation Twin-Boom Jet Fighter

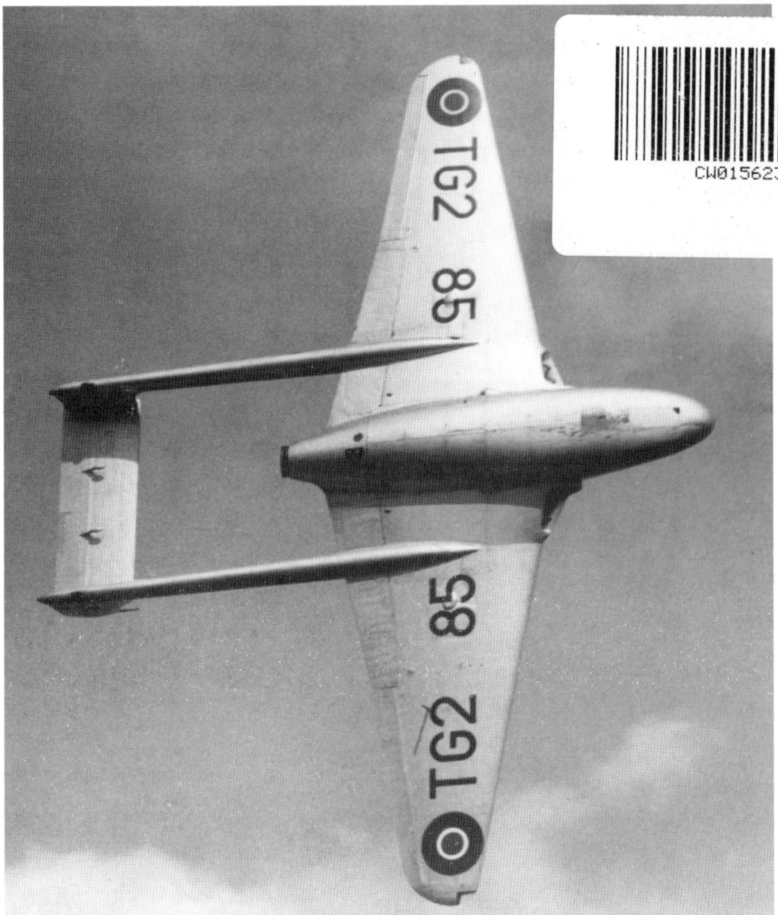

KEY Books

HISTORIC MILITARY AIRCRAFT SERIES, VOLUME 26

Front cover image: The pristine de Havilland Vampire T.11, WZ507, owned and operated by the Vampire Preservation Group at North Weald since 2005. (Darren Harbar Photography www.darrenharbar.co.uk)

Title page image: The twelfth of 120 Vampire F.1s built by English Electric at Preston and Samlesbury was TG285, which served the Royal Aircraft Establishment (RAE) and manufacturers before being transferred to the Royal Navy on 1 December 1947. Mainly involved in barrier trials, the Vampire was struck off charge (SOC) on 10 July 1950. (*Aeroplane*)

Contents page image: The familiar sight of a wet start as surplus fuel that has entered the tail pipe ignites in an impressive lick of flame. The aircraft was one of four Vampire F.1s ordered for the Swedish Air Force that preceded a much larger order for 70 examples, all redesignated as the J28. (*Aeroplane*)

Published by Key Books
An imprint of Key Publishing Ltd
PO Box 100
Stamford
Lincs PE9 1XQ

www.keypublishing.com

Original edition published as Vampire, De Havilland's successful, twin-boomed, first-generation jet fighter © 2014, edited by Martyn Chorlton

This edition © 2023

ISBN 978 1 80282 476 6

All rights reserved. Reproduction in whole or in part in any form whatsoever or by any means is strictly prohibited without the prior permission of the Publisher.

Contributors
Adrian Balch, Tony Buttler, Martyn Chorlton, Owen Cooper, Tony Haig-Thomas, David Oliver, John Perrot, Bertrand Rouillard, David H Smith

Typeset by SJmagic DESIGN SERVICES, India.

Contents

Introduction		4
Chapter 1	De Havilland's First-Generation Interceptor	5
Chapter 2	The Passerine Experimental	17
Chapter 3	Building de Havilland's First Twin-Boom Fighters	24
Chapter 4	Exceptional Versatility for Four Decades	32
Chapter 5	Vampires and Venom at War	41
Chapter 6	Handling the Vampire	47
Chapter 7	Advanced Training on Sir Geoffrey's Blood-Sucking Mammal	53
Chapter 8	Pioneering Jet-Powered Aerobat	59
Chapter 9	The Fleet Air Arm's Premier Jet Fighter	67
Chapter 10	Service in the World's Air Forces	74
Chapter 11	The Auxilliaries	80
Chapter 12	The 'Thin-Wing' Vampire	83
Chapter 13	Venom	91
Chapter 14	A Venom to Heaven	94
Chapter 15	All-Weather Sea Hornet Replacement	98
Chapter 16	The French North Winds Doth Blow	103
Chapter 17	Service in All Theatres	108

Introduction

Often completely overlooked in the grand history of aviation, the Vampire was the Royal Air Force's (RAF) second jet fighter and has always been overshadowed by the Gloster Meteor. With its code name of the DH.100 Spider Crab, the Vampire was, in fact, Britain's third jet to fly, Gloster also claiming the glory with the E.28/39. However, the Vampire took the honour of becoming the RAF's first single-engine jet fighter, and for a short time, the F.1, with a top speed of 540mph at 34,000ft, was the fastest. The early design trend was to incorporate a pair of jet engines into the design, owing to the lack of power that the early units produced and their lack of reliability. Once harnessed and fine-tuned, the jet engine quickly became a very reliable and powerful form of propulsion, especially for the later versions of the de Havilland Goblin, which gave pilots increased confidence in the aircraft. Below the surface of the Vampire's unique appearance was an aircraft that was easy to fly, easy to maintain and easy to build at home and under licence abroad. In fact, it achieved unprecedented orders from the moment it first appeared in RAF service.

After entering service too late to see action in World War Two, the Vampire remained at the forefront of RAF operational squadrons until the early 1950s, while the T.11 continued on in the advancing training role until the mid-1960s. With the Royal Navy, the Sea Vampire, again in the role of a trainer, served until 1970 and with foreign air forces, a few were still operationally active during the early 1980s. Switzerland retired its FB.6 target-tugs in 1990.

Along with the Meteor, the Vampire was the perfect 'first-generation' jet for the RAF. It was hugely popular with all who flew it but always ridiculed by those who had not, thanks to its almost toy-like appearance. Beaten to the interceptor role by the Meteor, the Vampire found its niche as a ground-attack aircraft, the machine reaching its developmental pinnacle as the FB.5. The Vampire also introduced many foreign air forces to jet aircraft, most significantly France, Sweden and Switzerland, all of which operated the type in large numbers and in different guises.

The story of the Vampire cannot be told without including the Venom and Sea Venom, which were developments of the original aircraft but redesigned to such an extent that they warranted a new company designation and name. These quite different machines continued the philosophy of a short pod-type fuselage and twin-boom layout, which continued, albeit in larger form, with the design of the Sea Vixen.

When 25 Squadron at West Malling received the Vampire NF.10 in July 1951, it became the world's first jet night-fighter unit. WP233, the second production aircraft, embarks on a nocturnal sortie. (*Aeroplane*)

Chapter 1
De Havilland's First-Generation Interceptor

Geoffrey de Havilland Junior (white shirt, sun glasses) looks on as the prototype de Havilland DH.100 Spider Crab, LZ548/G, is prepared for another flight from Hatfield in 1943. (*Aeroplane*)

Vampire origins

The de Havilland Vampire was originally known by its manufacturer's designation – DH.100; only later was it named Vampire. However, the story of Britain's second jet fighter really begins with a slightly earlier project called the DH.99 and the following information comes from the original DH.99 project brochure, dated 6 June 1941.

The aircraft proposal was described as a 'high altitude fighter with Halford engine', which referred to Frank Halford, who was responsible for designing the 2,900lb H.1 jet engine to be used by the aircraft. Like the Vampire, the DH.99 was a twin tail boom aeroplane, but it was to have an all-metal airframe and a single-spar wing with a D-nose torsion box and metal-covered ailerons and slotted flaps. The rudder empennage would go between the tail booms to ensure that there was no interference from the engine exhaust (which also avoided the necessity for a long tail pipe), a nose wheel tricycle undercarriage was employed and four belt-fed 20mm cannons were to be housed underneath the cockpit. The DH.99's span was 40ft and length 31ft, gross wing area 260sq.ft, normal weight 7,970lb and overload (with an armament of six cannons) 8,470lb.

The estimated maximum speed of the DH.99 using 2,700lb of the engine thrust was 445mph at sea level, 493mph at 35,000ft and 469mph at 45,000ft. Its rate of climb at sea level was 4,590ft/min and at 35,000ft it was 1,760ft/min; the time needed to reach 30,000ft was given as 9.6 minutes and the operational ceiling as 45,400ft.

The DH.99 brochure was criticised by Capt Liptrot at the Ministry of Aircraft Production (MAP) because it did not present sufficient detail. He considered the structure weight estimates to be optimistic and he had doubts about the performance estimates. However, in late July 1941, the Director of Technical Development, NE Rowe, made the decision to go forward with the new jet fighter. On 5 August of that year, Air Vice Marshal Sorley, Assistant Chief of the Air Staff, wrote 'we are ordering the design of a de Havilland fighter aircraft to accommodate a jet propulsion engine being built by Halford. The aircraft is to be a single-seater, four-cannon job.' By 11 November 1941, the project had been renumbered DH.100 and subsequently it used a structure of mixed wood and metal construction, with the pilot being housed in a wooden pod.

Specification E.6/41

Following the maiden flight of the Gloster E.28/39, powered by Frank Whittle's 'centrifugal flow' power plant in May 1940, jet-engine development progressed at a snail's pace as other higher priority war commitments took over. By 1943, Rolls-Royce and de Havilland began to produce improved versions of Whittle's ground-breaking design, which was rubber-stamped when the Meteor made its maiden flight on 5 March.

Prior to this, the Air Ministry had issued specification E.6/41 (OR.107) on 8 December 1942 calling for an 'experimental jet fighter'. The criteria for this new jet stated it should be a simply constructed, easy-to-operate and lightweight, single-engine fighter armed with four 20mm cannons. The earlier DH.99 had already come close to the specification and under the leadership of Chief Designer RE Bishop; the DH.100 was born.

Back in early 1941, the low power output of early British-designed jet engines meant that any future fighter would need at least two power plants to keep pace with the piston-engine machines of the day. The Meteor proved this theory, but the DH.100 would be a much smaller, lighter aircraft, designed around Frank Halford's H.1 centrifugal flow jet engine, which was more powerful than Whittle's earlier designs. Fitting the H.1 into a short fuselage would keep the jet pipe short, minimising loss of power. This was achieved by creating a twin-boom design with a pod fuselage containing the pilot, engine, armament and bulk of the fuel.

The Air Ministry was enthusiastic when presented with the design of the DH.100, and placed an order for two prototypes under contract SB/24539/C.23(a), at a cost of £40,000, on 11 April 1942. Three days later the order was raised to three prototypes, serialled LZ548, LZ551 and MP838, to be constructed at Hatfield. The latter location was approved as long as work on the DH.100 did not hinder the vital Mosquito production at that site.

DH.100

Progress on the DH.100 dragged on through 1942 because work on the DH.102 Mosquito took priority. By autumn, the DH.102 had been abandoned in favour of the DH.103 Hornet and all focus was back on DH.100.

Construction of the prototype DH.100s was undertaken in the Experimental Department at Hatfield under great secrecy. A distinctive looking aircraft from any angle, the jet also featured a short-legged, hydraulically-operated tricycle undercarriage with single wheels. The nose wheel retracted rearwards into the forward fuselage, while the main units retracted outwards and neatly concealed themselves into the lower wing.

The pilot was positioned as far forward as possible, which gave him an excellent forward field of vision. The prototypes and early F.1s were fitted with a three-piece canopy, but from the 87th production aircraft onwards, the familiar one-piece 'teardrop' canopy proved much better, especially

First flown by Geoffrey de Havilland Junior from Hatfield's grass runway on 1 September 1943, the prototype Spider Crab was powered by a 2,700lb Halford H.1 engine, later renamed the Goblin. (Via Martyn Chorlton)

for rear vision. The windscreen was fitted with armoured glass and could be de-iced with glycol. No ejection seat was fitted into the prototypes, or any of the single-seat aircraft and cockpit pressurisation was not introduced until the 51st production F.1 left the line. The pilot was also protected by armour plate behind his instruments and a panel was fitted behind his seat. Avionics were simplistic, consisting of a TR.1464 four-channel radio and an Identification Friend or Foe (IFF) set.

The DH.100s airframe was constructed of both wood and metal. The former was used in the fuselage from bulkhead number one to number four towards the rear, while the rest was made of metal. Developed from the construction of the DH.91 Albatross, this composite technique had several advantages, including reducing the airframe's weight, which improved performance and more practically, it helped to keep the cockpit warm. The fuselage was built in two halves just like the Mosquito, which were placed over interior contour wooden or cement moulds and once glued, were held together by flexible steel bands.

The wings of the DH.100 were tapered and fitted with outboard ailerons and inboard split flaps and like all of the flying controls, both were cable-operated via pulleys. The tail booms, tail unit and the wings were all made from flush-riveted aluminium. The intakes for the prototypes 2,700lb Halford H.1 (Goblin 1) were located at the wing roots, which had plates mounted on the side of the fuselage in front of the intake to stop the ingestion of stagnant 'boundary layer' air.

Spider Crab maiden flight

Work on the DH.100 gained momentum in 1943, but the jet fighter was not officially christened until 21 August, when the Director of Technical Development, NE Rowe, named the aircraft Spider Crab. Three days later, the first prototype, LZ548/G, was rolled out at Hatfield in readiness for taxiing trials. De Havilland Chief Test Pilot, Geoffrey de Havilland Junior carried out the preliminary taxi trials, although on each of the five runs conducted, the Spider Crab left the ground for at least 100 yards at a time.

The official maiden flight of LZ548/G came on 20 September 1943, once again with Geoffrey de Havilland Junior at the controls. The 30-minute flight ended with the de Havilland chief test pilot describing the aircraft as 'satisfactory' but over-balanced ailerons above 400mph and directional instability problems needed to be resolved.

The second prototype, LZ551/G, was first flown on 17 March 1944, and after initial trials was fitted with an arrester hook and transferred to the Royal Aircraft Establishment (RAE) at Farnborough where it served as the prototype for the Sea Vampire F.10 (a designation never officially adopted). The third

Photographs of the second prototype Spider Crab, LZ551/G, are frustratingly rare. This glimpse was taken prior to the aircraft's maiden flight on 17 March 1944. Note the lack of armament; a feature of the first two prototypes. (Via Martyn Chorlton)

prototype, MP838/G, was the first to be fitted with armament – four 20mm cannons – and also differed by having a Halford H.1A (same thrust as the H.1 but more robust and reliable) engine. MP838/G made its first flight on 21 January 1944 and by March was added to the strength of the RAE's Tactical Flight at Farnborough under the command of Wg Cdr HJ 'Willie' Wilson AFC. Part of Wilson's remit for running the Tactical Flight was to demonstrate and 'de-bunk' all preconceptions about jet flying and to do this he arranged for some of the top fighter pilots to fly the Spider Crab, including John Cunningham (later to work for de Havilland as chief test pilot), 'Sailor' Malan and David Atcherley. All of these experienced pilots' subsequent reports on the Spider Crab served de Havilland well when it came to fine tuning the production aircraft.

First production order: Vampire F.1

In April 1944, the Spider Crab was officially renamed the Vampire and by the following month a production order for 120 F.1s was placed with de Havilland. However, Hatfield was at capacity with increased Mosquito production and so the first Vampires built were subcontracted to English Electric at Preston. The Lancashire-based aircraft manufacturer was selected because of its excellent efficiency in producing the Handley Page Hampden and Halifax. Work began at the Strand Road Factory in Preston on 24 May 1944, with all Vampires being assembled and test flown from Samlesbury. The first production aircraft, TG274, flew from Samlesbury on 20 April 1945 and three days later was delivered to Hatfield for manufacturer's trials.

To speed up the Vampire's entry into service, the first 50 built were not fitted with a pressurised cockpit. A planned cockpit heated seat was also not fitted; instead warm air was extracted from a heater muff on the jet pipe via the gun-heating system. The F.1 was armed with four 20mm Hispano Mk V cannons mounted below the fuselage with provision for 150 rounds per gun (RPG). From TG336 onwards, the 50th aircraft, cabin pressurisation was installed with air supplied to the cockpit by a Marshall Type 6 blower, while the canopy was kept airtight by a Dunlop seal. The first 40 F.1s built were fitted with a Goblin 1 but from TG314 onwards a 3,100lb Goblin 2 was installed.

The Vampire F.1 entered RAF service with 247 Squadron in March 1946 at Chilbolton, replacing the Tempest F.2. The unit worked up quickly on its new jet fighters, taking part in the Victory Flypast over London on 8 June. In October 1946, 54 Squadron, which was also a Tempest F.2 unit, received the Vampire F.1, followed by 72 Squadron, which was reformed at Odiham on 1 February 1947; the two units created the RAF's first Vampire wing. The first Vampires to see service outside the country belonged to 3 Squadron at Wünstorf, West Germany, which relinquished its Tempest Vs for F.1s in

The fifth production Vampire F.1, TG278, built at Preston and first flown from Samlesbury en-route to Hatfield, photographed from an Albemarle in August 1945. De Havilland converted the Vampire to carry aerial cameras for a proposed photographic reconnaissance variant and later for Ghost engine development trials. (*Aeroplane*)

April 1948. The Royal Auxiliary Air Force (RAuxAF), which was destined to operate all marks of the Vampire in large numbers, received its first in July 1948 with 605 (County of Warwick) Squadron stationed at Honiley, replacing its Mosquito NF.30s.

The Vampire F.1 served for a relatively short period of time with 12 operational squadrons between March 1946 and June 1951 but was gainfully employed with second line units into the mid-1950s. Such was the Vampire's pace of development that the much-improved F.3 was in service a little over two years after the F.1.

Elephant-eared Vampire F.2

A separate chain of Nene-powered Vampires was born when three F.1 airframes, TG276, TG280 and TX807, were converted to specification F.11/45. The Nene was heavier than the Goblin but produced more power and, initially, the 4,500lb Nene RB.41 was installed by Rolls-Royce at Hucknall, in 1945. Designated as the F.2, the aircraft was easily recognisable because of the Nene's need for extra airflow, which was provided by a pair of prominent 'elephant's ears' auxiliary intakes on top of the fuselage.

A production order for 60 F.2s was placed by the RAF but this was cancelled by September 1945. Development work of the Nene-powered Vampire did not go to waste, however, as both Australia and France would produce their own variants with this engine installed.

Technical appreciation of the Vampire

On 11 January 1946, the Deputy Director of Aircraft Research and Development at the Ministry of Supply wrote a memorandum entitled *Technical Appreciation of the Vampire*, which provides a good summary for the stage of development that the aircraft had reached at the time. Some of the most interesting parts are given below, which shows quite strongly the support for a Rolls-Royce Nene-powered version, which became the Vampire F Mk II. The prototype TG276 flew with a Nene in March 1946.

- The Vampire is very shortly to be released for RAF use, and in addition it is an aircraft in which a number of foreign countries and the Dominions have expressed considerable interest; indeed some of them have already placed orders. It is wise, therefore, to examine the aircraft critically to assess whether it is likely to provide really useful service to both the RAF and other purchasers.

- The Vampire is well liked as a flying machine and has excellent flying characteristics over most of the speed range. Its behaviour at the highest speeds when it gets into the compressibility region is, however, not as good as some other fighters, notably the Supermarine Spitfire and Gloster Meteor. Moreover, for a jet-propelled fighter its critical Mach number, 0.76, is somewhat lower than other really advanced fighters. Above their critical Mach numbers, different types of fighter have experienced problems with compressibility in different ways. The Spitfire itself is noticeably innocuous in respect of buffeting and merely develops a nose-down pitching movement, while the Meteor gives good warning of compressibility by wing buffet together with a small amount of nose-up trim change. The Vampire, however, develops a fore and aft pitching oscillation which, if it is allowed to persist and is carried to higher speeds, can become violent and dangerous. It is clear, therefore, that pilots will have to recognise a very definite limit to the Mach number at which they may fly (the report noted that Mach number indicators were to be fitted when these had become available).
- In level flight and fitted with the 2,700lb thrust de Havilland Goblin I engine the Vampire will meet the compressibility limitation at approximately 520mph true air speed at 25,000ft. With the 3,000lb Goblin II the corresponding figure is 530mph at 18,000ft, and for the Rolls-Royce Nene that has been installed in a Mk.II Vampire (which it is expected will be cleared for the RAF at 4,500lb thrust) the aeroplane will be capable of level flight speeds of 10–20mph in excess of the compressibility limit (if it were possible to ignore the pitching oscillation). This means that in level flight the Nene Vampire will have to be flown throttled and the full benefit of the additional thrust made available by the Nene will show up in an improved rate of climb. At sea level the rate of climb should be above 7,000ft/min whereas the maximum rate of climb for the Goblin II is less than 5,000ft/min. In view of the insistence made by the air staff on very high rates of climb for interceptor fighters this is a clear advantage that the Nene Vampire enjoys.
- A great deal of research was done on the Vampire both in flight and by wind tunnel experiment to try and raise the critical Mach number, but we now conclude that short of redesigning the wings this is not possible. Separately, there has been some serious criticism from parts of the RAF in regard to the Vampire's engineering features, and solving these problems is now in hand with de Havilland.

Vampire F.3, VF345, served de Havilland as a demonstration aircraft in front of representatives from both the Australian and Argentine governments in 1948. Later allocated to 73 Squadron, the Vampire was damaged in a forced landing during a goodwill tour of Italy in September 1949, but it was later repaired and sold to the Italian Air Force. (*Aeroplane*)

Longer-range Vampire F.3

The Vampire F.1 suffered from the same age-old problem that had plagued interceptors from the outset; that of endurance. The F.1 could only remain airborne, on average, for just 45 minutes, although with a pair of underwing tanks this could be raised to two hours.

This problem was tackled in June 1945, when Vampire F.1, TG275, was delivered to Hatfield for installation trials under Modification Number 15. This modification involved fitting a new, long-range wing, which increased the fighter's internal fuel capacity to 330 gallons. This was achieved by placing four extra fuel tanks in the outer wing, which added 128 gallons. The original inner-wing fuel tanks were also upgraded to Marston-bag type, as were the new additional tanks.

A new type of external, pylon-mounted drop tank of 100 and 200-gallon capacity was also trialled under TG275. These additional cylindrical tanks, regardless of their capacity or shape, seriously affected the longitudinal stability of the Vampire and as such the tail structure was subjected to modification. The tailplane chord was increased by 4½in to 46½in, while the elevator chord was reduced by 1½in to 15½in. Large 'acorns' were also fitted where the tail plane and fin joined. The tailplane was also lowered by 13in, still above the jet efflux and the vertical tail surfaces were redesigned to a more rounded shape reminiscent of the earlier Moth, Rapide and Mosquito.

Powered by a 3,100lb Goblin 2 engine, TG275 was redesignated as the Vampire F.3 on 9 March 1946 but did not make its maiden flight until 4 November of that year. The modifications carried out on TG275 raised the gross weight from 8,578lb to 12,170lb, but the extra fuel capacity saw the fighter's range and endurance almost doubled when a full fuel load was carried.

TG275 was sent to the Aeroplane and Armament Experimental Establishment (A&AEE) at Boscombe Down in April 1947 for handling trials and clearance for service use. Contracts had already been signed and production orders placed with deliveries commencing from 22 April 1947. In early 1948, the Vampire Trials Unit conducted tests and tropical trials with VG702 and VG703, which were eventually flown back to Britain after undertaking a tour of the Middle East.

In the meantime, 54 Squadron at Odiham, under the command of Sqn Ldr RW Oxspring DFC, AFC, became the first operational unit to receive the F.3 in April 1948. At the same time, 'rumour control' at Odiham was reporting that the United States Air Force (USAF) was planning on crossing the Atlantic with its own new F-80 jets but the Air Ministry had other ideas. Well aware of the long-range capability of the F.3, it was decided that the RAF would cross the Atlantic before the USAF, and on 1 July 1948, six Vampires led by Oxspring left Odiham for Stornoway. Delayed by strong headwinds, the fighters arrived at Goose Bay, Canada, on 14 July and after carrying out demonstrations across that country, arrived at Andrews Field, Washington, on 25 July. The Americans had been beaten to flying the first

Originally ordered as Vampire F.3s, the last 18 aircraft (VF215–232) were built by English Electric at Preston as the first production FB.5s. After a spell with the Central Fighter Establishment, VF222 served with 93 Squadron in West Germany until the aircraft crash landed at Jever in February 1953. (*Aeroplane*)

jet aircraft cross the Atlantic, as the 56th Fighter Group and 16 F-80 Shooting Stars arrived at Odiham from Selfridge AFB on 21 July.

The Vampire F.3 served with 13 operational RAF squadrons including six auxiliary squadrons. It was with the latter that the type was retired from the front line in October 1952 when 605 (County of Warwick) Squadron at Honiley re-equipped with the Vampire FB.5. However, the F.3 served on with at least four second line units until March 1954.

The first of the fighter-bombers

When the Gloster Meteor was chosen as the RAF's main interceptor, de Havilland immediately set to work redesigning the Vampire for the ground-attack role. The Air Ministry was first drawn to the idea of a ground-attack Vampire in December 1946 and not long after, it issued Operational Requirement (OR) 237 for a ground-attack version of the F Mk IV to replace the Tempest.

The Nene-powered Mk IV stayed on the drawing board, but the FB.5 (first suggested as the Ground Attack (GA) Mk 5) was a ground-attack version of the F.3. Designed to specification F.3/47, modifications were to include increased fuel capacity, provision for a pair of 100-gallon drop tanks, a redesigned tailplane and bigger elevator trim tabs. The aircraft also had to be capable of delivering rockets and cannon fire in a dive or at low level and finally the specification called for the FB.5 to be fitted with an ejection seat. The latter request would cause de Havilland many headaches, mainly because the cockpit was only 22in wide and all ejection seats of the day would cause extensive alteration to the fuselage structure. The problem was first looked at in August 1946 when both Malcolm and Martin Baker seats were assessed; neither coming close to fitting satisfactorily. While the FB.5 would never be equipped with an ejection seat, the FB.6 in Swiss service and the Venom would, due to the early efforts made to overcome the problem.

All labour on the FB.5 ground to a halt in July 1947 following the death of Geoffrey de Havilland Junior and was not resumed until January 1948 when work began on converting ex-F.3 VT818 into a ground-attack prototype at a cost of £14,000. The prototype FB.5 completed its maiden flight from Hatfield on 23 June 1948. The FB.5 featured shorter wings, clipped by 12in, longer main undercarriage legs to provide clearance for under-wing stores, and power from a Goblin 2 engine.

The Vampire FB.5 entered RAF service with 16 Squadron at Gütersloh, West Germany, in December 1948, and replaced the Tempest F.2. In Germany, the FB.5 would become the backbone of the 2nd Tactical Air Force as well as taking over the role of the F.3 within Fighter Command.

The tradition of performing aerobatics with the Vampire was continued with the FB.5 by those units that had formed individual teams, such as 54 Squadron. The squadron demonstrated that the FB.5 was as good a performer as its predecessor when it put on an amazing display at Farnborough in July 1950 in front of the King and Queen. Not to be outdone, 16 Squadron became the first unit to fly jet fighters tied together.

The FB.5 became the first RAF jet fighter to serve in the Far East when 60 Squadron at Tengah, Singapore, re-equipped from the Spitfire FR.18 in December 1950. These aircraft would prove useful in the continuing fight against Communist terrorists, which had begun in 1948.

In the close-support role, the FB.5 finally relieved the Mosquito of this task and at its peak the definitive RAF Vampire equipped 40 squadrons including eleven auxiliary squadrons. It was with the auxiliaries that the type was retired from operational service in March 1957. But as with all former front-line aircraft there was always a secondary role in Flying Training Command, especially at Advanced Flying Schools and the School of Air Armament where the FB.5s ability to fire rockets was fully exploited.

Vampire FB.9s of 604 (County of Glamorgan) Squadron enjoy a two-week detachment from the home airfield at Llandow in Wales. These FB.9s, which are indistinguishable from the FB.5 at this angle, are seen off Gibraltar in August 1955. (Via Tony Buttler)

Cooling the 'hot box'

Responding to operational experience, especially from the large number of units now equipped with the Vampire across the Middle and Far East, it was decided to improve the FB.5 by tropicalizing it. Efforts to produce an effective air-conditioning system in the Vampire had been going on for quite some time in conjunction with the Institute of Aviation Medicine (IAM) at Farnborough. While de Havilland worked on a suitable air-conditioning system the IAM developed an air-ventilated suit system, which was first tested in FB.5, VV463, in May 1950, during trials from Khartoum, Sudan. For the cockpit, an air-conditioning unit made by George Godfrey and Partners Ltd of Hanworth, Middlesex, was mounted within the starboard wing root and the FB.9 was born.

Nicknamed 'Pike's Pig', the private-venture prototype Vampire NF.10, G-5-2, made its maiden flight in the hands of Geoffrey Pike from Hatfield on 28 August 1949. (Via Martyn Chorlton)

Following its delivery from Christchurch in 1951, Vampire NF.10, WP247, spent its short career with 23 Squadron at Coltishall and Horsham St Faith until January 1954. The aircraft remained on RAF charge, most likely in storage, until March 1958. (Via Martyn Chorlton)

In November 1951, the first FB.9s were ferried to the Mediterranean to re-equip 73 Squadron at Ta Kali, Malta, which was operating the FB.5. From early 1952, FB.9s began to be ferried in large numbers by Transport Command pilots to units in the Middle and Far East. On their return, the units' FB.5s were flown back to Britain to serve in a secondary role. The last single-seater variant of the Vampire to enter RAF service, the FB.9, served with 18 operational squadrons until the type was retired in March 1957 with the disbandment of 613 and 614 squadrons.

Private-venture interim night fighter

The first of the two-seater variants of the Vampire was not a trainer, as would be expected, but a night fighter, which was modified from the original aircraft to such a degree that it was redesignated as the DH.113. The aircraft was still undoubtedly a Vampire as the wings and twin-boom layout from the FB.5 were retained, but a completely new, longer fuselage pod was needed for the nocturnal role.

The fuselage was much wider than a standard Vampire because it had to accommodate two crew in a slightly staggered, side-by-side configuration just like a Mosquito. Even with a widened cockpit the seats were a snug fit; there was still not enough room to accommodate ejection seats and the only escape was to jettison the single-piece canopy. The pilot sat on the left and navigator/radio operator on the right, the latter controlling and monitoring an AI Mk X radar mounted in a bulbous, lengthened nose, which could be removed for access. The standard 20mm Hispano Mk V was retained in its original position with power provided by a Goblin 3 engine.

Two prototypes were constructed from company funds as the aircraft was not intended for RAF service because de Havilland was fully aware that the Meteor was already securing the night-fighter role. The first prototype, G-5-2, carried out its maiden flight from Hatfield on 28 August 1949 in the hands of Geoffrey Pike; the aircraft having already been christened as 'Pike's Pig'. Only nine days later, Pike demonstrated the DH.113 at Farnborough, where a great deal of overseas interest was shown in the aircraft. One customer, the Egyptian government, was so impressed it placed an order there and then for 12 DH.113s. However, tensions in the Middle East were on the rise again and the order was embargoed by the British government leaving the night fighters surplus. Rather than leaving de Havilland in the lurch, the order was taken over by the RAF, which redesignated the aircraft as the Vampire NF.10. These aircraft would complement the Meteor NF.11, speeding up the conversion to jets

The prototype Vampire T.11, with Class B registration G-5-7, captured not long after its maiden flight by John Wilson out of Christchurch on 15 November 1950. (Via Martyn Chorlton)

for the Mosquito crews and bridging the gap until the next generation of Meteor and Venom night fighters entered service.

The Vampire NF.10 entered RAF service with 25 Squadron at West Malling, in July 1952, making it the world's first jet night-fighter squadron. 23 Squadron at Coltishall followed in September and 151 Squadron, which reformed at Leuchars, in February 1952. The NF.10's service was predictably short, coming to an end in February 1954 when 25 Squadron re-equipped with the Meteor NF.12 and NF.14.

In total, 78 Vampire NF.10s were built and once the type was withdrawn from the night-fighter role, 36 of them were converted to NF(T).10 standard for navigation training. Modifications included removal of the radar from the nose, which was replaced with concrete ballast, and upgraded navigation equipment. The type served with 1 Air Navigation School (ANS) at Topcliffe and 2 ANS at Thorney Island until 1959.

Pioneering RAF jet 'wing' qualification

Prior to the arrival of a trainer variant of the Vampire, all RAF pilots concluded their advanced training and eventual 'wing' qualification on the piston-engine Harvard. As such, the fledgling pilot had no jet experience until he was posted to an Advanced Flying School (AFS) operating the tandem seat Meteor T.7. With the arrival of the Vampire T.11 this situation was improved, and from 1953 onwards the AFSs were closed down; pilots were now leaving the Flying Training Schools (FTS) with jet experience, which prepared them well for the final stage of their training at an Operational Conversion Unit (OCU).

Design of the Vampire T.11 began in spring 1950 under the de Havilland designation DH.115; its construction would be the responsibility of Airspeed and the de Havilland factory at Chester. The prototype, G-5-7 (later WW456), was first flown by John Wilson out of Christchurch on 15 November 1950. After a lengthy evaluation by the RAF, the Vampire T.11 was accepted to complement the Meteor T.7 already in service.

Based heavily on the Vampire NF.10, the T.11 featured a redesigned cockpit with the seats aligned side-by-side rather than staggered like the night fighters. The bulbous nose was retained for the aircraft's systems, which were accessed by a hinged bonnet-type panel. Fitted with dual controls, the T.11 was equipped with four 20mm cannon as per the operational single-seaters, plus it had the capability to carry external stores. After entering service, it was discovered that the NF.10-type canopy was not great for visibility. Continuous complaints about the lack of ejection seats were finally addressed from the 144th aircraft off the production line. A one-piece canopy dramatically improved visibility and the fitment of a pair of Martin-Baker Mk 3B ejection seats gave renewed confidence to all who flew in the T.11. The aircraft's general handling was also improved with redesigned fins.

The Vampire T.11 entered service with 206 Squadron at Valley, detached from Oakington, and 209 Squadron at Weston Zoyland. The T.11 joined 5 FTS at Oakington in 1954, the first course on the type beginning in May. Oakington was the first RAF station to introduce the later stage of flying training at which students graduated on the Provost at Ternhill and continued on to the T.11. The 5 FTS T.11 syllabus involved 110 hours of training made up of dual instruction, aerobatics, instrument flying, navigation exercises, night flying and formation flying.

The RAF College at Cranwell received its first T.11s in 1956, replacing the Balliol, the first jets to serve with the unit. The type also served with 4 FTS at Worksop, 7 FTS at Valley and 8 FTS at Swinderby, all in large numbers. In January 1958, 7 FTS was soaked up by 1 FTS at Linton-on-Ouse to form the RAF's first combined basic and advanced flying training school. The introduction of the Folland Gnat in 1959 saw a gradual withdrawal of the T.11 from FTSs, but several lingered on with 3 FTS at Leeming until 1967. On 29 November 1967, four T.11s carried out the last operational sortie, rounded off by an impressive aerobatic display before landing at Leeming.

A few T.11s remained in service with the Air Traffic School at Shawbury until 1969, leaving the Central Flying School (CFS) at Little Rissington as the last bastion for the type. From 1972, the CFS formed a new aerobatic team flown by pilots from the unit's examining wing, named the Vintage Pair. T.11 XH304 teamed up with a Meteor T.7 until 1986 when both were lost in a mid-air collision at Mildenhall. The loss of XH304 brought the long career of the Vampire T.11 in RAF service to a sad conclusion.

Vampire F.3, VF345, strikes an immaculate pose during its time as a de Havilland demonstrator specifically for the benefit of the Australian and Argentine governments. Later transferred to 73 Squadron, the aircraft was damaged at Bergamo, Italy, on landing and was eventually transferred to the Italian Air Force. (*Aeroplane*)

Chapter 2

The Passerine Experimental

De Havilland DH.108, VW120, the third prototype being joined by Vampire F.1, TG278. (*Aeroplane*)

Planning ahead

As early as 1943, the designers at de Havilland began to study the feasibility of a very advanced civilian airliner potentially powered by four Goblin turbine engines. By the end of the year, the design had evolved into a 20-passenger machine, with a similar layout to the Vampire fighter, but with all the engines grouped around the tail. By August 1944, the design was modified into the Vampire Mail Carrier powered by three Ghost engines. This aircraft reached the model stage and was tested in the Royal Aircraft Establishment (RAE)'s wind tunnel at Farnborough. One month later, it was officially designated by de Havilland as the DH.106; the Comet was born.

The DH.106 was still a long way from its final form and in October 1945 the design team, now led by Ronald Bishop, proposed that the aircraft could have a swept wing and no tail. With an all-up weight of 75,000lb, the aircraft now appeared, on paper at least, as a 24-seat airliner powered by four Goblin engines. In order to reduce the weight of the wing structure and drag in the cruise, a 40-degree sweepback was incorporated into the wing and the engines were now positioned under the trailing edge of wing. By this time, it was clear that an experimental aircraft would be needed to trial a wing with such a dramatic sweepback and a separate team, led by John Carver Meadows Frost, began working on what would become the DH.108. In the meantime, the DH.106 featured a tail from 1946 and the well-known shape of what was to become the world's first commercial jet airliner began to take hold.

Half-scale model

Design work on the DH.108 was already at an advanced stage when the project was given some weight by the Air Ministry, which issued OR.195, specification E.1/45 for a pair of experimental tailless research aircraft in support of the DH.106 airliner. The remit was later fine-tuned to specification E.11/45, still for two aircraft, but one was to be built to explore low-speed handling and the other to test the high-speed handling of the swept wing. A development of the Vampire F Mk 1, the DH.108's specification had three, clear main objectives: to carry out full-scale experiments into high-speed flight; to gather detailed aerodynamic and structural measurements; and to operate as a half-scale version of the DH.106.

Ordered under contract SB.66562, dated 13 December 1945, the two prototype DH.108s, unofficially named Swallow by the Ministry of Supply (MoS), were to be serialled VN856 and VN860. Instead, a pair of Vampire F Mk 1 fuselages, serialled TG283 and TG306, were taken off the English Electric production line at Preston and serials VN856 and VN860 were duly cancelled in February 1946.

TG283 would be the first prototype and was designed with low-speed handling in mind. Powered by a 3,100lb Goblin 2 engine, the original Vampire fuselage was lengthened and covered in light alloy. A pair of all-metal wings with a 43-degree sweep, complete with a set of Handley Page slats on the outer leading edge of the wing, locked in the open position, were fastened to the fuselage. The wing would restrict the top speed of TG283 to 280mph. A conventional swept single fin and rudder were fitted at the rear of the fuselage while elevons (a combined elevator and aileron) were fitted to the trailing edge of the outer wing and large split trailing-edge flaps were mounted inboard. No ejection seat was fitted because of the cost and delay it would have caused the test programme.

During the construction of TG283, the RAE issued a report to de Havilland regarding wind-tunnel testing of the swept-wing design. The report described how there was a high probability of the aircraft entering a 'Dutch roll'.* As a failsafe, de Havilland installed a pair of anti-spin parachutes into cylindrical-shaped pods mounted on each wing tip.

* A combined rolling and yawing oscillation, which could result in total loss of control especially at low speeds.

The first of three DH.108s built, TG283, pictured at Hatfield in October 1946. (Via Martyn Chorlton)

Woodbridge debut

On 5 May 1946, the diminutive DH.108, TG283, was taken by road to Woodbridge, Suffolk, which had a long wartime emergency runway. With chief test pilot Geoffrey de Havilland Junior at the controls, a high-speed taxi run turned into a quick hop, prior to the wheel brakes overheating on 11 May. Once the brakes were replaced, the first DH.108 made its maiden flight on 15 May 1946. After landing, the test pilot praised the handling qualities of the aircraft especially at low speeds and was quick to point out that there was no hint of a Dutch roll.

High-speed prototype

The second DH.108, TG306, designed to evaluate the high-speed characteristics of the swept-wing, differed from the first aircraft in several ways. The sweep of the wing was increased to 45 degrees and the Handley Page leading-edge slats were now automatic. The pilot's seat was lowered to compensate for a stronger metal-framed canopy and powered flying controls of the same type planned for the DH.106 were installed. A 3,350lb Goblin 3 engine was fitted, giving the second DH.108 the potential to fly comfortably at 650mph.

TG306 completed its maiden flight, once again in the hands of Geoffrey de Havilland Jr., from Hatfield on 23 August 1946. The following month, TG306 made its public debut at the Society of British Aircraft Constructors (SBAC) display at Radlett, where Geoffrey de Havilland Jr put on an outstanding performance for the crowd in the little swept-wing aircraft.

Even though de Havilland had already committed to the DH.108 research programme, the company began to have doubts about a design with a heavily swept-wing and no tail. The whole design of the DH.106 was suddenly brought into doubt, but it was already clear that the DH.108 had the potential to be a record breaker and, as such, sights were set on the world speed record. On only its fourth flight, TG306 had reached Mach 0.89 (677mph); the world record was 616mph at the time, held by Gp Capt 'Teddy' Donaldson in a Gloster Meteor.

The second DH.108, TG306, with Geoffrey de Havilland at the controls, not long after its maiden flight in August 1946. (*Aeroplane*)

Some of the remains of TG306 on the mudflats of Egypt Bay off All Hallows-on-Sea on the Isle of Grain on 28 September 1946, the day after Geoffrey de Havilland lost his life during a high-speed dive from 10,000ft. (Via Owen Cooper)

One tragic test flight

The official course for a world speed record run was off the south coast near Tangmere. Geoffrey de Havilland had already conducted several promising trial runs. On 27 September 1946, Geoffrey de Havilland took off at 17.30 in TG306 from Hatfield for another simulated record attempt after a high Mach 0.87 (662mph) run was performed over the Thames Estuary. This was to be the last test flight before he flew down to Tangmere for the record attempt. This initial test was to continue the investigative work into the behaviour of swept wings. On reaching 10,000ft, TG306 was entered into a dive to investigate controllability. In an instant, at approximately 5,000ft, the aircraft suffered a violent structural failure and disintegration. It is believed at one point the aircraft had reached Mach 0.90 (685mph) before both wings failed at their root-end attachment points, forcing them to fold rearwards. The wreckage was spread over a one-mile-long path on mudflats north of Egypt Bay, not far from All Hallows-on-Sea on the Isle of Grain.

Geoffrey de Havilland Jr. OBE was killed instantly by a violent blow to the back; his body was found nearly 20 miles further down the coast at Whitstable on 7 October. He was buried in Tewin Churchyard, near Welwyn, alongside his brother, John, who was killed flying a Mosquito on 23 August 1943.

The show must go on

Despite the loss of his second son, Sir Geoffrey de Havilland announced in November 1946 that research work with the DH.108 would continue. At the same time, former-night-fighter pilot John Cunningham was given the job of chief test pilot (engines).

In an effort to improve the performance of the DH.108, high-altitude engine trials and testing of a new streamlined and strengthened canopy were undertaken using Vampire F.1, TG281. A redesigned, slightly longer and pointed nose was also trialled using Vampire F.1, TG443 and combined with the improved canopy it was obvious that the DH.108 could fly faster with these modifications. Other changes included power-boosted elevators, a modified cockpit complete with an ejection seat and a 3,750lb Goblin 3 engine; the latter being more than capable of pushing the DH.108 into supersonic territory. To apply these modifications, a replacement for TG306 was needed and on 10 July 1947, a contract was issued for a third DH.108, to be serialled VW120, with power provided by a 3,738lb Goblin 4. Constructed at Hatfield from a Vampire FB.5 airframe, VW120 made its maiden flight from Hatfield in the hands of John Cunningham on 24 July 1947.

The first prototype, TG283, presents a good view of its 43-degree sweep wing and Handley Page leading-edge slats, which were fixed open. This aircraft gave valuable service until its untimely demise on 1 May 1950. (Via Owen Cooper)

Record breaker

The performance of the third DH.108 was encouraging to such an extent that de Havilland decided to have a crack at the FAI Class C.1/1 100km International Closed-Circuit Speed Record, which in April 1948 was held by Mike Lithgow in his Supermarine Attacker at 564.88mph. On April 12, de Havilland experimental test pilot, John Derry, took off in VW120 in an attempt to break the record. Following a pentagonal-shaped course laid out from Bell Bar near Hatfield, via Puckeridge, Arlesey, Sundon and Redbourne, Derry smashed the record with a speed of 605.23mph.

Derry continued to raise the bar in VW120, becoming the first British pilot to exceed Mach 1.0 on 6 September 1948; a feat he repeated in the same aircraft on 1 March 1949. Both of these breaches of the sound barrier were 'hairy' flights, which began in a steep dive from 40,000ft and were only recovered by using the DH.108's trailing-edge trim flaps. Data gathered during both Mach 1.0 flights showed that VW120 had not decelerated to sub-sonic speed until thicker air was reached at 26,000ft.

Before VW120 was transferred to the RAE, the DH.108 took part in the SBAC Challenge Trophy Race in 1949, achieving a third place finish. (Via Owen Cooper)

Further trials and tragedy

The first prototype, TG283, was handed over to the RAE at Farnborough in October 1948 to continue a wide range of test flying. One of the more interesting trials that TG283 took part in was conducted during February and March 1950. The DH.108 was used to assess high angle-of-attack, low-speed landings and to prevent damage being caused to the jet-pipe, TG283 was fitted with a Sea Vampire undercarriage with a longer stroke. This meant that the undercarriage had to be permanently locked down because there was not enough room in the bays to accommodate it.

Unfortunately, TG283 was lost on 1 May 1950 during sideslip and stalling trials with the Officer Commanding Aero Flight, Sqn Ldr GEC 'Jumbo' Genders AFC, DFM, at the controls. After successfully executing one clean stall at 15,000ft, Genders entered a second stall with the flaps down but immediately lost control and TG283 entered an inverted spin. At 8,500ft, the anti-spin chutes were deployed, but the starboard parachute jammed and once down to 7,500ft, Genders jettisoned the port chute, most likely because it was proving ineffective. At 5,000ft the cockpit canopy was jettisoned and

DH.108 VW120 pictured after transfer to the RAE in July 1949 where it would conduct high-speed trials until its loss on 15 February 1950. (*Aeroplane*)

at 2,000ft control of the DH.108 was temporarily recovered moments before the aircraft entered a final, unrecoverable normal spin. Genders attempted to bail out at this point but was unable to pull his rip-chord before he struck the ground with a partially streamed parachute trailing behind him. TG283 came down near Hartley Wintney in Hampshire in an upright position.

VW120 concluded its de Havilland flight trials on 28 June 1949 and was also transferred to the RAE at Farnborough to undertake high-speed longitudinal stability and aero-elastic distortion at high Mach number trials. It was during one of the latter trials that VW120 was lost with the Officer Commanding Aero Flight, Sqn Ldr JSR Muller-Rowland DSO, DFC, at the controls on 15 February 1950. The trial was planned to take place at 38,000ft, but at 27,000ft the DH.108 suddenly began to rapidly descend before completely disintegrating at 10,000ft. Although the initial enquiry concluded that the pilot had become incapacitated by a faulty oxygen system, the most likely cause was divergent longitudinal oscillations, a type of instability the DH.108 was prone to. The bulk of the wreckage of VW120 came down at Brickhill, near Bletchley in Buckinghamshire.

So ended a period of British flight testing, which contributed significantly to the development of the swept-wing but sadly at the price of three pilots' lives. Between May 1946 and May 1950 the three Swallows had accumulated 480 test flights and a plethora of technical data and knowledge that would be put to good use in the future.

The third and final DH.108 'Swallow' prototype was VW120, ordered to replace TG306, which claimed the life of Geoffrey de Havilland Junior on 27 September 1946. VW120 was first flown by John Cunningham (at the controls in this image) from Hatfield on 24 July 1947. (*Aeroplane*)

Chapter 3

Building de Havilland's First Twin-Boom Fighters

An impressive view of the main production hangar at de Havilland's Chester/Broughton factory, where 979 Vampires were built. Note integrated production of de Havilland Chipmunks. (*Aeroplane*)

De Havilland Aircraft Co, Hatfield, Herts

Prototypes (3)   LZ458/G (f/f 20 Sep 1943), LZ551/G (f/f 17 Mar 1944) and MP838/G (21 Jan 1944)
DH.108 (3)   TG283 (f/f 15 May 1946), TG306 (f/f 23 Aug 1946) and VW120 (f/f 24 Jul 1947)
Vampire FB.5 (32)   VZ808–838 and VZ840, delivered between 1 Jul 1949 and 29 Mar 1951
Vampire NF.10 (3)   G-5-2 (f/f 28 Aug 1949), G-5-5 and G-5-9
Vampire T.11 (114)   WZ453, WZ460, WZ464–466, WZ496, WZ472–474, WZ478, WZ496, WZ503–505, WZ571, WZ573–575, ZD453, XD458–459, XD509, XD531–532, XD541, XD550–551, XD595–603, XD627, XE820, XE822, XE830, XE848–-862, XE868–871, XE885–889, XE893–897, XE919–921, XE928–937, XE942–961, XE991–998 and XH271–274 delivered between 29 Jan 1953 and 30 Aug 1955

A few of the 75 Vampire FB.6s, serialled J-1005 to J-1079, pictured at Hatfield in late 1951. (Via *Aeroplane*)

Vampire FB.6 (75)	J-1005–1079 for Switzerland, delivered between 1 Apr 1949 and 29 Apr 1950
Vampire FB.52 (5)	V0047 B-BG, V0062 B-BB, V0074 B-BC, V0076 B-BD and V0098 B-BE for Norway, delivered between 10 Dec 1949 and 16 May 1950
Vampire FB.5 (4)	For Venezuela, delivered 1949/1950
Vampire FB.52 (28)	1500–27 for Egypt, delivered between Mar 1950 and Mar 1955
Vampire J.28B (22)	28148C, 28203C, 28213C, 28217–218, 28227, 28237–238C, 28247C*, 28248C, 28252, 28253C*, 28254–257, 28259C*, 28261–262, 28265–266 and 28271C* (*C = finished at Chester) for Sweden, delivered between May 1950 and Mar 1951
Vampire FB.52 (39)	HB732–770 for India, delivered between Sep 1950 and Mar 1951
Vampire FB.52 (10)	For Italy; delivered as components for assembly by Fiat in Nov 1950
Vampire NF.54 (2)	S3-167–168 for Italy, delivered on 4 Jun 1951
Vampire FB.52 (9)	336–341 and 3890150391 for Iraq, delivered between May 1953 and Nov 1955

Total Hatfield Production = 349

De Havilland Aircraft Co, Hawarden/Broughton, Chester

Vampire FB.5 (67)	VZ839, VZ841–852, VZ860–877, WG793–807, WG826–837, WG840–847 and WL493, delivered between 30 Mar 1951 and 12 Nov 1951
Vampire FB.9 (225)	WL493–518, WL547–587, WL602–616, WP990–999, WR102–158, WR171–180, WR182–186, WR189–204, WR207–211, WR213–231, WR233–236, WR238–242, WR244–249, WR253–255, WR259–266, WX208–212, WX214–215, WX222–223 and WX242, delivered between 2 Nov 1951 and 13 Mar 1952. (WR265, WR268, WX212, WX215 and WX223 were delivered to Marshalls on 12/13 March 1953 for completion)
Vampire NF.10 (55)	WM660–677, WM703–733, WP250–252 and WV689–691, delivered between 27 Nov 1951 and 13 Jun 1952

Vampire T.11 (257)	WZ454, WZ457–459, WZ461–463, WZ467–471, WZ475–477, WZ495, WZ497–498, WZ500–502, WZ510–521, WZ550–570, WZ576–593, WZ607–620, XD376–377, XD379, XD388–392, XD425, XD430, XD434, XD437, XD439–441, XD452, XD455–457, XD463, XD506–508, XD526, XD528–530, XD534–540, XD542–549, XD552–554, XD588–593, XE821, XE827–829, XE832–833, XE885, XE890–892, XE922–927, XE938–941, XE976–990, XK582–590 and XK623–637
Vampire T.55 (3)	G-ANVF, G-AOXH and G-APVF, all private venture, later sold to Finland, Chile and Lebanon respectively
Vampire J.28B (9)	28148, 28203, 28213, 28238, 28247, 28248, 28253, 28259 and 28271 for Sweden, delivered between 10 May 1950 and 16 Mar 1951 (all finished at Chester)
Vampire FB.52 (25)	B-BF to B-BO and B-CA to B-CR for Norway, delivered between 12 May 1950 and 15 Mar 1951
Vampire FB.52A (51)	S3-156 to S3-166 and S3-171 to S3-210 for Italy, delivered between 27 Jul 1950 and 6 Dec 1951
Vampire FB.52 (10)	211–220 for South Africa, delivered from Apr 1951
Vampire FB.52 (18)	NZ5721–5738 for Royal New Zealand Air Force (RNZAF), delivered between 10 Apr 1951 and 15 Feb 1952
Vampire T.55 (43)	IY467–470 and IY514–552 for India, delivered between 12 May 1953 and 14 Apr 1954
Vampire NF.54 (12)	S3-169 to S3-220 for Italy, delivered between 22 Jul 1952 and 25 Mar 1953
Vampire FB.5 (20)	S3-156 to S3-166 and S3-171 to S3-210 to Venezuela, delivered 1952
Vampire FB.52 (6)	VA-1 to VA-6 for Finland, delivered from 16 Jan 1953
Vampire FB.9 (30)	227–256 for South Africa, delivered from Apr 1953
Vampire T.55 (10)	28431–28440 for Sweden, delivered between Aug and Nov 1953
Vampire T.55 (4)	L151, L154, L159 and L160 (ex-G-APFV) for Lebanon, delivered between 24 Aug 1953 and 2 Nov 1957
Vampire T.11 (3)	U1001–1003 for Switzerland, delivered between 15 Sep 1953 and 14 Jan 1954 (all converted to T.55 standard in 1960)
Vampire FB.52 (4)	L152–153, L155–156 and L158 for Lebanon, delivered between Oct 1953 and Mar 1955
Vampire T.55 (5)	334–335 and 386–388 for Iraq, delivered between Dec 1953 and 20 Sep 1955
Vampire T.55 (5)	J.01–J.05 for Chile, delivered between 29 Dec 1953 and 1 Jun 1954 including T.55 G-AOXH (later J.01)
Vampire T.55 (21)	257–277 for South Africa, delivered between Feb 1954 and 17 Jun 1955
Vampire T.55 (5)	CF501–505 for Ceylon, delivered by sea between 25 Jun 1954 and Jul 1954 but contract cancelled and aircraft returned to Chester still inside their crates. CF501–503 were later resold to Finland as VT-4, VT-3 and VT-2 respectively
Vampire T.55 (8)	UB501–UB508 for Burma, delivered between 30 Nov 1954 and 22 Feb 1955
Vampire T.55 (12)	1570–1581 for Egypt, delivered between 28 Jun 1955 and Feb 1956
Vampire T.55 (9)	VT-1 to VT-9 for Finland, delivered between Jul 1955 and Mar 1956. VT-1 ex-15485/G-ANVF; VT-2 ex-CF-503; VT-3 ex-CF-502 and VT-4 ex-CF-501
Vampire T.55 (8)	J-701 to J-708 for Indonesia, delivered between 21 Sep and 28 Oct 1955
Vampire T.55a (15)	28441–455 for Sweden, delivered between 25 Oct 1955 to Feb 1956. Became SK.28C-2 in Swedish Air Force service

Vampire FB.52 SA219 makes its way by crane from the main assembly hall at Chester to the paint shop in March 1951. (Via *Aeroplane*)

Vampire T.55 (1)	15752/G-5-14/63-5571 for Japan, delivered 19 Nov 1955
Vampire T.55 (7)	U-1004 to U-1010 for Switzerland, delivered between 13 Jan and 26 Jun 1956
Vampire T.55 (6)	185–187 and 191–193 for Ireland, delivered between 5 May 1956 and 16 Mar 1961
Vampire T.55 (2)	493 and 494 for Syria, delivered to Hatfield on 24 Jul 1956 because order was embargoed
Vampire T.55 (5)	5C-YA to 5C-YC, 5C-YR and 5C-YS for Austria, delivered between 26 Mar 1957 and 25 May 1961
Vampire T.55 (13)	BY377–386 for India, delivered between 5 Oct 1957 and 6 Feb 1958. BY996-998 assembled from components by Hindustan Aircraft Ltd, Bangalore
Vampire T.55 (5)	2E-35 to 6E-35 for Venezuela, delivered from 30 May 1958

Refurbished aircraft
Vampire T.55 (5) for India; Vampire NF.10 (30) for India as NF.54; Vampire T.55 (3) for Austria; Vampire T.11 (9) for Switzerland and a Vampire T.55 '333' for Iraq (the latter was to be modified with ejection seats by HSA at Chester but the aircraft returned with fuselage of XH316 instead.

Total Chester Production = 979

De Havilland Aircraft Co, Christchurch, Hants

Vampire T.11 (1)	Prototype G-5-7 (f/f 15 Nov 1950) later WW456
Vampire T.11 (2)	Pre-production aircraft, WW458 and WW461, later delivered to Royal Navy, 21 Jan 1952 and 22 May 1952, respectively. WW461 later evaluated as T.22
Vampire T.11 (123)	WZ414–430, WZ446–456, WZ493–494, WZ499, WZ506–509, WZ544–549, XD375–387, XD395–404, XD424, XD426–428, XD431–432, XD442–443,

	XD449–451, XD454, XD460–462, XD510–525, XD533, XD606–607, XD625–626, XE816–819, XE823–826, XE831, XE863–867 and XE872–883 delivered between 1 Mar 1952 and 11 Mar 1955
Sea Vampire T.22 (73)	XA100–131, ZA152–172, XG472–748 and XG765–777, delivered between 26 May 1952 and 25 May 1955
Vampire T.55 (6)	NZ5701–5706 for RNZAF, delivered between 29 Apr and 15 Dec 1952
Vampire T.55 (6)	221–226 for South Africa, delivered between 26 May and 29 Sep 1952
Vampire T.55 (6)	PX-E, PX-G, PX-M, ZK-X, ZK-Y and ZK-Z for Netherlands, delivered between 25 Jun and 10 Nov 1952
Vampire T.55 (1)	2A-36 for Venezuela, delivered 16 Sep 1952
Vampire T.55 (2)	5801 and 5802 for Portugal, delivered 30 Oct and 4 Dec 1952
Vampire T.55 (1)	333 for Iraq, delivered 25 Mar 1953
Vampire T.55 (20)	28411–430 for Sweden, delivered between 7 Feb and 2 Jul 1953
Vampire T.55 (1)	L151 for Lebanon, delivered 26 May 1953

Total Christchurch Production = 242

English Electric Co, Preston, Lancs

Vampire F.1 (154)	TG274–315, TG328–355, TG370–389, TG419–448, VF265–283 and VF300–314, delivered between 23 Apr 1945 and 3 Dec 1946
Vampire F.II (1)	TX807, delivered 21 May 1947
Vampire F.3 (138)	VF315–348 (VF362–392 re-serialled VG692–732), VG692–703, VT793–835, VT854–874 and VV187–214 (VV209–211 to India; VV212–214 to Norway), all delivered between 22 Apr 1947 and 7 May 1948. (VF317 converted to Sea Vampire; VF315 to F.20 and VG701, VT795 and VT802–805 converted to F.21)
Vampire FB.5 (788)	VV215–232, VV443–490, VV525–569, VV600–640, VV655–700, VV717–736, VX461–464, VX471–476, VX950–990, VZ105–155, VZ161–197, VZ206–241, VZ251–290, VZ300–359, WA101–150, WA159–208, WA215–264, WA271–320, WA329–348, WA355–404, WA411–460, WE830–849, WF578–579 and WF584–586, delivered between 24 May 1948 and 23 Oct 1951. (The following were converted to Sea Vampire, VV215, VV548, VV631, VV635, VX973, VZ142–143, VZ145–146 and VZ148)
Vampire FB.5 (18)	VV136–153, delivered to Hatfield for Sea Vampire F.20 conversion, carried out between Jun and Sep 1948
Vampire FB.9 (42)	WG848–851, WG865–892 and WG922–931, delivered between 19 Nov 1951 and 19 Feb 1952
Vampire F.1 (70)	28001–070 for Sweden as J.28A, delivered between 4 Jun 1946 and 18 Aug 1947
Vampire F.1 (4)	J1001–1004 for Switzerland, delivered between 29 Jul 1946 and 25 Jul 1947
Vampire F.3 (86)	17001–042 and 17044–086, delivered to Canada between 30 Sep 1947 and 13 Feb 1948
Vampire FB.5 (10)	201–210 for South Africa, delivered between Jan and Mar 1950

Total Preston Production = 1311

English Electric at Preston built more Vampires than any other manufacturer including the RAF's first F.1s. TG292 is in the foreground, one of a batch of 154 by English Electric and delivered between April 1945 and December 1946. (Via David H Smith)

Fairey Aviation Co. Ringway, Manchester

Vampire FB.9 (51)   WR181, WR187–188*, WR205–206, WR212, WR232, WR237, WR243, WR250–252, WR256–257, WR267–269, WZ201–207, WZ213, WZ216–221, WZ224–241, WZ259–260 and WZ339–342, delivered between 13 May 1952 to 30 Nov 1953. WX261–308, WX327–376, WX403–435, WX459–487 all CNX. WX219, WX228, WX231, WX233, WX235–242 and WX260, all transferred to South Africa

*WR187 renumbered from WX340, and WR188 renumbered from WX341

Vampire T.11 (30)   XD393–394, XD403, XD435–436, XD444, XD448, XD594, XD604, delivered between 5 Jul 1954 to 11 Oct 1955

Vampire FB.52 (1)   256 to South Africa, delivered to Chester 29 May 1953

Vampire FB.52 (3)   342–344 to Iraq, delivered to Hatfield 25 and 26 August 1953

Vampire FB.52 (4)   L152–L153 and L155–L156 to Lebanon, delivered to Chester between May and Dec 1954

Vampire FB.52 (7)   1524 and 1530–1535 to Egypt, delivered to Chester between 7 Sep 1954 and 11 Jan 1955

Vampire FB.52 (1)   CF510 for Ceylon, delivered to Chester 12 Jul 1954

Total Ringway Production = 97

Marshall of Cambridge (Engineering) Ltd

Vampire T.11 (2)   XD429 and XD438 delivered 30 Mar and 26 Mar 1954, respectively

Total Marshall Production = 2

De Havilland Aircraft Pty, Ltd, Bankstown, Sydney, NSW, Australia

Vampire F.30 (57)	DHA 4001–4057, delivered to RAAF between Sep 1949 and Jul 1952. DHA 4030–4057 (28) were retrospectively modified to FB.31 standard by 1956
Vampire FB.31 (23)	DHA 4058–4080, delivered to RAAF between Sep 1952 and Aug 1953
Vampire T.33 (36)	A79-801 to A79-836 (DHA 4081–4121), delivered to RAAF from Oct 1952
Vampire T.35 (1)	A79-600 (ex-A79-836) prototype
Vampire T.35 (68)	A79-601 to A79-668 (DHA 3122/4131, 4133/4190), delivered to RAAF between Sep 1957 and Jun 1960
Vampire T.34 (5)	A79-837 to A79-841 (DHA 4105–4109) for RAN from 1954
Vampire T.34A (1)	A79-842, delivered to RAN 8 Mar 1957

Total Bankstown Production = 191

Hindustan Aircraft Ltd, Bangalore, India

Vampire FB.52 (247)	IB200–IB1707 and BB431–BB448, the first HAL aircraft flying on 21 Feb 1952
Vampire T.55 (60)	IY1591–IY1600 and BY390–BY478 delivered to Indian Air Force from circa 1958

Total Hindustan Production = 307

A pair of Iraqi Air Force Vampire FB.52s, 390 and 391 pictured in the snow at Hatfield in November 1955 prior to delivery. (Via *Aeroplane*)

Société Nationale de Constructions Aéronautiques du Sud-Est, Marignane, Marseilles, France

SE.532 Mistral (4) 01*–04 pre-production aircraft, delivered between Jun 1950 and Oct 1951.
  *f/f (first flown) 1 Apr 1951
SE.535 Mistral (247) 1–247 production variant, delivered between Jun 1953 and Feb 1954

Total Sud production = 251

Federal Aircraft Works (F+W), Emmen, Switzerland

Vampire FB.6 (100) J-1101–200 for Swiss Air Force, delivered between Mar 1951 and Nov 1952
Vampire T.55 (20) U-1011–030 for Swiss Air Force, delivered between Jul 1958 and Jun 1959

English Electric built 1,311 Vampires of various marks at its Preston and Samlesbury factories in Lancashire, from 1945 to the mid-50s. These Vampires are a few of the 816 FB.5s built by English Electric. Note the de Havilland Sea Hornets and Devons in the background. (*Aeroplane*)

Chapter 4

Exceptional Versatility for Four Decades

DH.100 Spider Crab

Designed to specification E.6/41, three prototype DH.100 Spider Crabs were built, serialled LZ548, LZ551 and MP838. These aircraft had tall-pointed fins while production variants were square-cut.

Engine	2,700lb Halford H.1, H.1A and 3,100lb Goblin 1
Span	40ft
Length	30ft 9in
Height	9ft
Wing area	266sq/ft
Weight	5,898lb
AUW	8,000lb
Max speed	490mph
Range	580 miles

Vampire F.1, TG275 puts on a typically spirited display for the period at the 1948 SBAC at Farnborough in 1948. Two Vampire FB.5s and a Vampire F.3 were also present at that year's display. (*Aeroplane*)

Six Vampire F.3s of 601 (County of London) Squadron out of North Weald sometime between September 1949 and September 1952. While the majority of auxiliary squadrons re-equipped with the Vampire FB.5, 601 Squadron bucked the trend and received the Meteor F.8 instead. (*Aeroplane*)

Vampire F.1

The first production Vampire F.1 single-seat fighter, TG274, made its maiden flight at Samlesbury on 20 April 1945. The first 40 aircraft built were fitted with the Goblin, while subsequent machines were powered by the Goblin 2. Other modifications from the 40th production airframe included provision for drop tanks under the wings. Pressurisation was introduced after the initial 50 aircraft had been built and the original three-piece canopy was replaced by an improved bubble hood.

Engine	3,100lb Goblin and Goblin 2
Span	40ft
Length	30ft 9in
Height	8ft 10in
Wing area	266sq/ft
Weight	6,372lb
AUW	10,298lb
Max speed	540mph
Ceiling	40,000ft
Range	730 miles

Vampire F.2 and Mk IV

The Vampire F.2 (or F.II) and the projected F.4 were powered by the Rolls-Royce Nene, each being characterized by a pair of elephant's ears intakes positioned above the engine, directly behind the cockpit. Two aircraft, TG276 and TG280, both F.1s were taken from the production line in April 1945 and allocated to Rolls-Royce Hucknall. The conversion work on TG276, under specification F.11/45, began in June 1945, followed by TG280 in September.

Despite the results of any trials not being received, an order for 60 F.2s was placed in February 1945. Later reduced to 40 aircraft – two F.2s and 38 Mk IVs – the contract was ultimately cancelled in September 1945. A third aircraft, TX807, was also built as an F.2; this machine later being delivered to Australia to serve as the prototype F.30.

Engine	4,500lb Nene RB.41
Span	40ft
Length	30ft 9in
Height	8ft 10in
Wing area	266sq/ft
Weight	7,762lb
AUW	13,448lb
Max speed	575mph
Ceiling	49,000ft
Range	1,118 miles

Vampire F.3

The prototype Vampire F.3 single-seat fighter made its maiden flight on 4 November 1946. It differed from its predecessor by having a greater fuel capacity. This increased from 202 to 326-gallons, bolstered by the provision to carry either 100 or 200-gallon auxiliary fuel tanks. The F.3 also had its tail unit modified with lower fins and rudders, which gave a much more rounded contour. These modifications raised the loaded weight to 11,970lb, but the ability to carry more fuel meant that the range was increased to 1,390 miles when maximum fuel was carried.

Engine	3,100lb Goblin 2
Span	40ft
Length	30ft 9in
Height	8ft 10in
Wing area	266sq/ft
Weight	7,134lb
AUW	11,970lb
Max speed	531mph
Ceiling	43,500ft
Range	1,050 miles

Vampire FB.5

The first fighter-bomber version of the Vampire was the Goblin 2-powered FB.5, the prototype of which, VV213, made its maiden flight on 23 June 1948. The main features of the FB.5 were a 2ft-shorter span with squared-off tips and a longer-stroke undercarriage. The latter was necessary to cope with the increased sink rate caused by the much higher all-up weight of the aircraft. The increased weight arose because of the strengthened wings, which were now capable of carrying rockets and bombs.

Engine	3,100lb Goblin 2
Span	38ft
Length	30ft 9in
Height	8ft 10in
Wing area	262sq/ft
Weight	7,253lb

AUW	12,360lb
Max speed	535mph
Ceiling	40,000ft
Range	1,145 miles

Vampire FB.6

Designed as a single-seat fighter-bomber, the Vampire FB.6 came about because of the international interest being shown in the FB.5. The Swiss government placed an order for 75 aircraft to be powered by the Goblin, and following trials in June 1947, it was designated as the FB.6 in August. Later built under licence in Switzerland, orders were also placed by Sweden, which designated the aircraft as the FB.50 and in service the J.28B. In total, 12 FB.6s were converted into target presentation aircraft in 1978, featuring a Venom-style nose. The main export version of the FB.6 was the FB.52, which is covered separately.

Engine	3,350lb Goblin 3
Span	38ft
Length	30ft 9in
Height	8ft 10in
Wing area	262sq/ft
Weight	7,283lb
AUW	12,390lb
Max speed	548mph
Ceiling	42,800ft
Range	1,220 miles

Vampire FB.8

Designed to specification F.15/49, issued in March 1948, for a 'thin-wing' production version of the Vampire, this aircraft was powered by a Ghost. In a contract that was worth £180,000, two FB.5s, VV612 and VV618 were transferred from Preston to Hatfield and converted into FB.8s. The subsequent redesign was so extensive, a completely new aircraft type was born in the shape of the DH.112 Venom.

Vampire FB.9

By the early 1950s, the Vampire was in widespread service with the RAF including units based in the Middle and Far East. To help cope with these harsh environments it was decided to produce a variant more suited to tropical climates. The result was the FB.9, which featured a fully air-conditioned cockpit powered by a Godfrey cabin-refrigeration plant buried into the wing. This installation resulted in a slightly different wing plan form in which one fillet was eight inches longer than the other.

Engine	3,100lb Goblin 2
Span	38ft
Length	30ft 9in
Height	8ft 10in

Wing area	262sq/ft
Weight	7,283lb
AUW	12,390lb
Max speed	548mph
Ceiling	42,800ft
Range	1,220 miles

Vampire Mk 10 (DH.113)

The first two-seater Vampire began life as a private venture designated as the DH.113, which was designed to be used as a night-fighter. Making use of the wings and tail of an FB.5, the DH.113 was given a new, longer fuselage providing sufficient room in the nose for an AI Mk X radar and side-by-side seating for a pilot on the left and navigator on the right. The crew seats had to be staggered as there was not much room and with no ejection seats fitted, the only escape was via a hinged canopy, which could be jettisoned.

Two prototypes, G-5-2 and G-5-5, were built by de Havilland; the first nicknamed Pike's Pig made its maiden flight from Hatfield on 29 August 1949 with Geoffrey Pike at the controls. A third Mk 10, G-5-9, joined the test fleet in August 1951. After being displayed at Farnborough in September 1949 the first prototype attracted an order from Egypt for 12 aircraft, which was later embargoed by Britain. This order was taken over by the RAF, which redesignated the aircraft as the NF.10.

Vampire NF.10

A two-seat night-fighter variant, the Vampire NF.10 entered the RAF to serve alongside Meteor NF.11 units. It was also introduced to accelerate the re-equipping of the night-fighter force, which was still operating Mosquitoes. When 25 Squadron at West Malling received the type in July 1951, it became the world's first jet night-fighter unit. By 1954, the Vampire NF.10 was already being superseded by the Meteor NF.12 and NF.14 and the Venom NF.2.

Engine	3,350lb Goblin 3
Span	38ft
Length	34ft 7in
Height	6ft 7in
Wing area	262sq/ft
Weight	6,984lb
AUW	11,350lb
Max speed	538mph
Ceiling	40,000ft
Range	1,220 miles

Vampire NF(T).10

Following the withdrawal of the NF.10 from the night-fighter role, 36 aircraft were selected for conversion into navigation trainers. Redesignated as the NF(T).10, modifications included removal of the AI Mk X radar, which was replaced by concrete block ballast and upgraded navigation equipment.

Vampire Mk 11 Trainer (DH.115)

The private venture DH.115 was a prototype two-seat, dual-controlled jet trainer, which would enter RAF service as the T.11. The prototype, serialled G-5-7 (later WH456), made its maiden flight from Christchurch on 15 November 1950. Very similar in overall design to the DH.113, the Vampire Trainer was not fitted with radar or ejection seats in the early production aircraft.

Vampire T.11

The first production T.11, WW458, initially flew on 1 December 1951, this aircraft being delivered to the Royal Navy, while the first RAF machine was WZ414. Not long after the first batch of T.11s was delivered, modifications were implemented including a one-piece, moulded-cockpit canopy, which gave a better field of vision. Dorsal fairings were added in front of the fins along the tail booms, and ejection seats were also fitted later in the production run.

Engine	3,350lb Goblin 3
Span	38ft
Length	34ft 7in
Height	6ft 7in
Wing area	262sq/ft
Weight	7,380lb
AUW	11,150lb
Max speed	538mph
Ceiling	40,000ft
Range	840 miles

Vampire F.30

The first Vampires to be built in Australia were the Nene-powered F.30. John 'Blackjack' Walker conducted the maiden flight on 29 June 1949. The first 57 of 80 built featured the same elephant's ear intakes on the upper fuselage as the F.2 but following issues with high-speed handling, these were repositioned to the lower fuselage. The remaining 23 of this batch were built as FB.31s.

Engine	5,000lb Nene 2-VH
Span	38ft
Length	30ft 9in
Height	8ft 10in
Wing area	262sq/ft
Weight	7,600lb
AUW	11,000lb
Max speed	538mph
Ceiling	40,000ft
Range	840 miles

Vampire FB.31 and F.32
The Australian-built, Nene-powered FB.31 featured stronger wings with squared-off tips very similar to the FB.5. Only one aircraft was converted to FB.32 standard, which involved larger intakes, an ejection seat and an air-conditioned cockpit.

Vampire T.33 and T.34/T.34A
Powered by a Goblin 35, the Australians produced three different trainer variants, beginning with the T.33, which were constructed to the same specification as the RAF's T.11. The T.34 followed, of which only five were built to the same standard as the early Sea Vampire T.22 to train crews for the Sea Venom all-weather fighter. Upgraded later, these five aircraft were redesignated as T.34As.

Vampire T.35
The T.35 was similar to the T.33/34 family but was constructed to the same specification as the later production RAF T.11s, compete with one-piece canopies and ejection seats. Several T.33s were converted to this specification, these aircraft being designated as T.35A.

Engine	3,500lb Goblin 35
Span	38ft
Length	30ft 9in
Height	6ft 7in
Wing area	262sq/ft
Weight	7,380lb
AUW	11,680lb
Max speed	538mph
Ceiling	40,000ft
Range	787 miles

Vampire FB.50 (J.28B)
This was the export classification for the FB.6s ordered by Sweden, which were redesignated in Swedish Air Force service as the J.28B. Twelve of the 310 constructed were later rebuilt as T.55s.

Vampire FB.51
Built under licence by Sud-Est, the FB.51 was effectively an FB.5, which was assembled in France with British components. The first of 67 Goblin-powered Vampires supplied in component form made its maiden flight from Marignane on 27 January 1950.

Vampire FB.52 and FB.52A
The main export version of the FB.6 was the successful FB.52, of which 193 were sold to ten countries between December 1949 and October 1953. In total, 353 FB.52s were also built under licence in Italy

and India and another 51 FB.52As were supplied to the Italian Air Force from Chester between July 1950 and December 1951. A further 27 FB.52As were also licence-built by the Macchi Company in Italy.

Engine	3,350lb Goblin 3
Span	38ft
Length	30ft 9in
Height	8ft 10in
Wing area	262sq/ft
Weight	7,283lb
AUW	12,360lb
Max speed	548mph
Ceiling	42,800ft
Range	1,220 miles

Mark 53 (SE.530/532/535 Mistral)

The Mistral was a development of the French-built FB.51, which was first flown on 21 December 1950 by test pilot Jacques Lecarme. The most significant change was the powerplant, a 5,000lb Hispano-built Nene 102, which was supplied through larger intakes rather than being assisted by the original elephant's ears design. The aircraft, initially designated as the Mark 53 by de Havilland, and the SE.530 Mistral by Sud-Est, also had an increased fuel capacity and a pressurized cabin. Four prototypes were built, the first of them flying on 1 April 1951, again in the hands of Jacque Lecarme.

The Vampire entered production without ejection seats as the SE.532, but from the 94th aircraft onwards ejection seats were fitted as standard and the following 150 were designated as the SE.535. The SE.535 was powered by a Nene 104 and also featured several minor modifications. The majority of SE.532s were retro-fitted with ejection seats, the first of them being put to the test on 23 January 1953 when Jean Boulet became the first Frenchmen to use one.

Engine	5,000lb Nene 102B and 104 (Hispano-Suiza-built)
Span	38ft
Length	30ft 9in
Height	8ft 10in
Wing area	262sq/ft
Weight	7,656lb
AUW	12,628lb
Max speed	568mph
Ceiling	44,000ft
Range	1,220 miles

Vampire NF.54

The export version of the Vampire NF.10 was the NF.54 of which 14 'new-build' aircraft were sold to Italy between 1951 and 1953. The designation was also applied to 30 former RAF NF.10s, which were refurbished for the Indian Air Force and delivered between 1954 and 1958.

Vampire T.55

The export version of the DH.115 Trainer, the T.55 was another success story, with more than 200 built from scratch and a further half dozen converted from T.11s. The T.55 was also built under licence in Switzerland and India, the latter converting several of its aircraft to PR.55 standard.

Engine	3,500lb Goblin 35
Span	38ft
Length	30ft 9in
Height	6ft 7in
Wing area	262sq/ft
Weight	7,380lb
AUW	11,680lb
Max speed	538mph
Ceiling	40,000ft
Range	787 miles

Vampire FB.9, WL559 'P', WR236 and WL586 of 8 Squadron over Aden in 1953. WL559 was transferred to 7 Flying Training School (FTS) and WL586 to the Lebanese Air Force in June 1958, while WR236 only served with 8 Squadron, which operated the FB.9 from Khormaksar, Sheikh Othman, Nicosia, Deversoir, Habbaniyah, Eastleigh and Khartoum between December 1952 and July 1955. (*Aeroplane*)

Chapter 5

Vampires and Venom at War

Malaya Operations

In December 1950, 60 Squadron, based at Tengah on Singapore Island, converted from Spitfires to the Vampire FB.5. The first operational jet sortie of Operation *Firedog* was a strike against Communist Terrorist (CT) positions on 26 April 1951, and by June the new jets had flown a total of 214 sorties. Although they were popular with the ground crews, the Vampires were seriously affected by heat and humidity, which restricted their operations. Pilot Ken Cooke of 60 Squadron gave his first impression of the Vampire FB.5.

> The Vampire was a useful aircraft for the bandit-bashing role. Armament was four 20mm guns in the nose, and it could carry 2,000lb of bombs and usually four 60lb warhead rockets. It was an extremely stable platform for weapon delivery and did not have the marked trim changes in the dive exhibited by the Spitfire FR.18 with its huge five-bladed propeller, acting like a powerful gyroscope causing control inputs to be processed through 90 degrees.
>
> Forward visibility was excellent, a great change after the huge nose of the Griffon-engine Spitfire. In the ground-attack role in the mountain area of Malaya the advantage that the Spitfire had was to be able to stand on its tail quickly and claw its way upwards, particularly useful when operating in

60 Squadron Vampire FB.5s over Singapore in 1951. Operating from Tengah, the unit operated the Vampire FB.5 and FB.9 from December 1950 to August 1955, followed by the Venom FB.1 and FB.4 until November 1959. (*Aeroplane*)

Above: A trio of 8 Squadron Vampire FB.9s over Aden in 1953, which operated from Khormaksar. The squadron operated in the Middle East from September 1946 to December 1967. (*Aeroplane*)

Left: A No. 32 Squadron Venom FB.4 in Cyprus. (David Oliver Archives)

valleys when the mountain tops were covered in clouds. It was not very often that we had precision targets such as camps or buildings to attack. These were always popular as the skills earned on the range were used to effect. It was a bit irritating to get the usual target of 10,000 to 20,000 square yards of jungle at which to shoot rockets knowing that your own personal accuracy was less than three yards average error including a high percentage of direct hits.

The Vampire 5 was a pleasant and easy aircraft to fly but really under powered. We called it the 'whistling kiddicar'. The Mk 9 was even more pleasant as it had cockpit air-conditioning, a real boon in Malaya. The other feature was a Lear radio compass housed under a white plastic cover in the nose. It was, however, unreliable during my time with the squadron and not much use.

Middle East operations

The Vampire FB.9 saw extensive action in the Middle East where those of 8 Squadron, having replaced its Bristol Brigands at the end of 1952, and 32 Squadron, operated against dissident tribes in the Wadi Habib region of the Aden Protectorate. This was part of six-month long Operation *West Bard*, during which 8 Squadron flew a total of 1,130 sorties against various rebels in the Western Protectorate. In May 1953, the squadron's Vampires took part in Operation *Alergio* flying 12 sorties with two 500lb bombs against Dar Marabel.

French Air Force Mistral 535s of Escadre 1/6 operated over Algeria between 1955 and 1961. (David Oliver Archives)

In April 1954, a detachment of four FB.9s of No 8 Squadron arrived at Eastleigh in Kenya, from where they flew 160 anti-Mau Mau sorties using rockets and cannon during the following four weeks. The Vampire detachments in Kenya continued until April 1955.

North African action

Meanwhile, France's Armée de l'Air had re-equipped with 157 Vampire FB.5 plus 251 Nene-powered variants built by Sud Aviation and known in the service as the Mistral. Three Mistral units, Escadre 1/6 at Oran, 1/7 at Bizerte and 1/8 at Rabat, operated against Algerian rebels between 1955 and 1958. The Mistral featured a more powerful engine, an ejection seat and a CGS gun-sight. Lt Col Georges Grousset flew the Mistral 535 with Escadre 1/6 for three years in Algeria:

14 Squadron RNZAF Venom FB.1s took part in Operation *Firedog* in Malaya. (David Oliver Archives)

Against trees, huts and men sometimes, we used eight big US T.10 rockets, 500lb bombs, 20mm cannon with 800 rounds, and napalm. As a fighter, it was a good one. It was the last anyway, for the pilot alone. After the Mistral, the ground forces took control of every action. But the Mistral's main drawback in Algeria was that it was short of fuel at low altitude, so it was used for ground support only after the rebels were practically surrounded.

The Venom

The Vampire's successor, the DH Venom, was initially designed as an interceptor with an excellent rate of climb and good manoeuvrability, but it is best remembered as a rugged ground-attack aircraft. Powered by the DH Ghost, the Venom FB.1 suffered a number of teething troubles, which delayed its entry into service until 1953, first in Germany, then two years later in the Middle East and Far East.

In the Middle East, the first Venom FB.1s began replacing 8 Squadron's Vampires in May 1955. In July, the squadron flew 80 sorties against rebels in Wadi Habib in the Aden Protectorate. At the same time, in Malaya, 60 Squadron's newly delivered Venoms were taking part in Operation *Smash Hit*, during which four aircraft were held on standby to scramble within five minutes for anti-CT strikes in the Johor area. By the end of the year, 45 and 14 Squadrons of the RNZAF had re-equipped with the FB.1, while the improved FB.4 variant was being introduced to Middle East squadrons. Air Marshal Sir David Harcourt-Smith flew Venoms with 8 Squadron from September 1955 to the end of 1957:

I had flown the Venom Mk 1 on my previous tour with the 2nd Tactical Air Force in Germany and, shortly before I arrived at Khormaksar in Aden, 8 Squadron re-equipped with the Venom Mk 4. I recall the major change was that the Mk 4 had powered flying controls and was probably the first swept-wing/power-controlled aircraft of British design to enter service with the RAF. In addition, the Mk 4 had a much greater range capacity.

My logbook records that I flew 81 operational sorties in the Aden Protectorate. The majority of these sorties were convoy escort, border patrols or operations in support of what was known as the Proscribed Area Policy, in simple terms preventing dissidents from entering certain areas of the Protectorate. The aircraft's armament was usually six or eight 3in rockets and two guns, or from time to time, in place of the rockets we carried two 1,000lb bombs. It was unusual for the squadron aircraft to suffer any damage from enemy fire, although I recall on a couple of occasions suffering minor damage from small-arms fire.

Sea Venom FAW.21 of 893 Squadron, damaged by flak and with an injured navigator on board, makes a successful belly landing on the flight deck of HMS *Eagle* during the Suez campaign. (Via Martyn Chorlton)

My tour in Aden was interrupted by a squadron detachment to Cyprus for about five months during which time we took part in the ill-fated Suez campaign. From 1 to 6 November 1956, I flew ten sorties out of Akrotiri against Egyptian airfields at Fayid, Abu Sueir and Kabrit, as well as sorties against what remained of the Egyptian Army, mainly in the form of soft-skin vehicles and tanks.

Opposition, albeit only from the ground by the Egyptians, was a good deal more intense and effective than from Aden rebels. It was not unusual to return from Egypt with damage from enemy ground fire. Some was substantial but the fact that we did not lose a single aircraft through enemy action speaks volumes for the robust nature of the Venom. No 8 Squadron claimed 43 aircraft destroyed on the ground plus a further six probables during Operation Musketeer.

I thoroughly enjoyed the Venom. It was a pleasant aircraft to fly, an excellent weapons' platform as well as being a rugged fighting machine.

The Fleet Air Arm joins the fray

Another variant of the Venom family, the Fleet Air Arm's (FAA) DH Sea Venom, also saw action in support of Operation *Musketeer*. A navalised development of the RAF Venom NF.2, a two-seat, all-weather, day or night fighter, the Sea Venom FAW.21 was able to carry comparable weapons load to that of the Venom, and four squadrons of Sea Venoms took part in the Suez campaign in the ground-attack role. 891 and 893 squadrons flew from the aircraft carrier HMS *Eagle*, while 809 and 895 squadrons, equipped with the more powerful FAW.22, operated against Egyptian airfields and military installations from the carrier HMS *Albion*. Only one aircraft was hit by anti-aircraft fire, an FAW.21 belonging to 893 Squadron, which belly-landed on *Eagle* with an injured navigator on 1 November.

Shortly before it was disbanded in April 1958, 809 Squadron flew a number of strikes against Ethniki Organosis Kyprion Agoniston (EOKA) in Cyprus from HMS *Albion*, while two years later, 891 Squadron Sea Venoms flew 21 rocket sorties against Yemeni guerilla hideouts in the Aden Protectorate from HMS *Ark Royal*.

1958 was a year of turmoil in Southern Arabia, with a state of emergency being declared in Aden when Yemeni forces occupied Jebel Jehaf. RAF Venoms were in the thick of the action from day one of the emergency, attacking Yemeni forces at As Sarir and Qa'tabah and losing three aircraft to ground fire in the process. At the same time, a revolt was breaking out in Oman and a detachment of 8 Squadron operating from Sharjah against rebel strongholds, lost one Venom to ground fire. In January 1959, the Squadron's aircraft supported an SAS force that broke the back of the rebellion and a month later No 8 Squadron returned to Khormaksar where its Venom FB.4s were replaced by Hunter FGA.9s in January 1960.

Rhodesia

Following a brief lull in RAF operations, FAA Sea Venoms from HMS *Ark Royal* carried out a number of rocket strikes against dissident mountain tribesmen during Operation *Damon* in April 1960, which was the last time that a British Venom variant was used in action.

However, in 1965, Rhodesia made a Unilateral Declaration of Independence (UDI) and Vampire FB.9s of 2 Squadron Rhodesian Air Force went on to operate against nationalist guerillas for the next few years. They were supplemented by 11 former South African Air Force FB.52s after UDI. In February 1964, the final flight of the Vampire FB.9 was undertaken by the commanding officer of 2 Squadron.

Operating alongside the FB.9s on anti-guerilla operations during UDI were a dozen Vampire T.55s. Although designed primarily as an advanced jet trainer, the two-seat T.11 was armed with two 20mm cannons and could carry a selection of underwing stores including rockets or two 500lb bombs. In 1969, No.2 Squadron carried out reconnaissance flights over the western, northern and eastern borders using Vampire T.55s. The squadron also took over a counter insurgency commitment and the defence and ground-attack role, until the country achieved independence in 1980 as the Republic of Zimbabwe.

Left: Rhodesian Air Force Vampire FB.9s and T.11s of No 2 Squadron were used in anti-guerilla operations after UDI. (David Oliver Archives)

Below: A quartet of Vampire FB.5s of 72 Squadron at North Weald in the spring of 1950. After reforming at Odiham in February 1947, the squadron had progressed from the Vampire F.1 and F.3 before the first FB.5s arrived in November 1949. From July 1952, the squadron began the slow conversion to the Meteor F.8, seemingly reluctant to part with its Vampires, which were not withdrawn until May 1953. (*Aeroplane*)

Chapter 6
Handling the Vampire

A pair of RAF standard advanced trainer Vampire T.11s go tail chasing 'over the top' at altitude from an Operational Conversion Unit (OCU) during the early 1950s. (Via Martyn Chorlton)

Vampire incident, 1 September 1953
Vampire FB.5, VZ190 of 229 Operational Conversion Unit (OCU) from Chivenor, flown by Plt Off P J Perrot collided with FB.5, WA403, also of 229 OCU, flown by Plt Off RG Rooke during battle-formation training. Both aircraft came down off Hartland Point, Devon; Perrot escaped by parachute and was later rescued; Rooke, aged 20, was killed. John Perrot describes the incident:

Aircraft down off Hartland Point
The collision was no more than a jolt; not unlike a nudge from the car behind you at the traffic lights. Glancing left, my wing-man's Vampire FB.5 appeared in full plan view, cockpit uppermost, and close in on the port side. In an instant it was gone, and my aircraft flicked hard right into the tightest and fastest spin I have seen, before or since.

Through the windscreen, the Bristol Channel beneath me appeared to be rotating at an incredible rate, and to be very close. This was an illusion; the collision occurred at 26,000ft and for the first 8,000ft of the tumble to earth I worked to get out of the cockpit.

I pulled the cockpit canopy jettison handle. Nothing happened. The cockpit pressurisation system used an inflatable seal to close the gap between the canopy and the fuselage, and it had to be deflated before the Perspex hood could be opened. I turned off the seal and tried the jettison handle again. The effect was startling. I neither saw nor heard the canopy go, but go it did, and in an instant.

Releasing the straps was an instinctive move. As the aircraft continued relentlessly rolling down to the sea it produced alternately positive 'G', which held me down in my seat and negative 'G', which tended to throw me out. I remained tied to the aircraft by my radio lead, which in the days of leather helmets was not of the quick-release type. Jerking out the plug, I kicked the seat and the next moment I was falling clear of the aircraft.

Photographs of 229 OCU Vampires are surprisingly rare considering how many examples passed through the unit. This is FB.5, VX977 'P' of 229 OCU displaying the later 'RS' unit code. The Vampire remained with the unit until 1957. (Via Martyn Chorlton)

At the time of the impact the aircraft was flying at 300kt. The human body, falling free, does so at about 120kt. When baling out, therefore, one ought to wait for the body to slow down before opening the parachute. This, I regret, I omitted to do. The parachute opened with great violence and I carried bruises from the harness for a long while afterwards. The sky appeared empty and only the sound of the wind was to be heard. The sea below appeared uninviting and on the horizon I could see the north Devon coastline.

The excruciatingly slow descent into the Bristol Channel took nearly a quarter of an hour. Cold, frightened and very lonely I gave no thought as to what had happened to my aircraft. The Vampire, having lost its twin tail booms in the collision, had slowly disintegrated during its wild descent. By the time it reached the water its break-up was complete and finally it vanished beneath the waves. Vampire FB.5 VZ190 lies there to this day.

During the descent I had the unusual experience of looking down on another Vampire. The pilot was, in turn, looking down at the sea for me, not realising how slowly I was falling.

Successful belly-landing

This was my second accident in a Vampire FB.5. Earlier, a main undercarriage leg on WA415 obstinately stayed up when the other two legs were lowered. No amount of recycling the gear or pulling positive 'G' would make the third wheel come down, and shortage of fuel added to my problems. The only solution was to land on the grass of the airfield with all wheels retracted. The Vampire landed at about 80kt so the moment of touchdown was quite exciting. After the initial impact I was convinced that the nose of the aircraft was going to dig in and cause the Vampire to turn head over heels onto its back. In the event this fear came to nothing; with a brief jolting slither the aircraft came to rest, little the worse for the experience. The problem turned out to have been caused by a broken bolt in the undercarriage mechanism. The underside of the fuselage suffered minor damage during the landing but was quickly repaired and seven days later it was flying again.

Superstition says accidents always happen in threes; for a long while afterwards I subconsciously waited the third.

Vampires and I were destined to meet many times over a period of several years. Our first encounter was at a busy airfield on Anglesey (RAF Valley), the peaceful air of which was frequently

The most prolifically produced of all the Vampire variants, the FB.5 introduced hundreds of pilots to their first taste of the freedom and power of flying a single-seat jet fighter. (Via Martyn Chorlton)

shattered by the peculiarly penetrating whistle of the Goblin engine. As a pupil pilot, it was the first British jet aircraft with which I was entrusted. Fresh from the apparently endless skies of Texas and the sophistication of the Lockheed T-33, it seemed a simple, even rudimentary machine in comparison. Its cockpit was more reminiscent of wartime practice than of the jet age.

Appearances were deceptive though, for it proved to be very much a pilot's machine – light, responsive and a good gun platform. It gave many years of faithful service to the RAF in its various guises of front-line fighter, advanced trainer and night fighter. It was the second British operational jet fighter (the first was the Meteor) but it arrived just too late to see action in World War Two. In the late 1940s and early 1950s the single-seat version was operated by the RAF worldwide. The two-seat version was developed from it, one form of which served as the standard RAF advanced trainer right into the 1960s, the other as a night fighter.

A friendly cockpit

Aircraft cockpits, in my experience, reflect the personality and qualities of the aircraft. Sitting for the first time in a Tempest, that large and brutal piston-engined fighter, surrounded by an apparently haphazard arrangement of struts, switches, gauges, controls and warning notices, my impression was 'This brute is out to kill you.' The Vampire FB.5, however, displayed no such tendencies. The pilot sat well down in the fuselage, looking through the long, deep front windscreen. The cockpit was small but fairly uncluttered and the whole effect was friendly. No ejection seat was fitted and although I suppose this had an adverse effect on safety, it did make for a more comfortable ride.

Some mental agility and a head for figures were needed to calculate the fuel state. This was shown on five separate gauges clustered behind the stick, which had the conventional 'spade grip' of the time.

In the early days, before the two-seat version came into service, no dual instruction was possible. To pilots used to operating large tail-wheeled, piston-engined fighters, the apparent complexities of using a nose wheel and a turbine provided food for thought. Standard practice was to sit the pilot in the cockpit and then detail a number of the largest and heaviest ground-crew to drape themselves over the twin tail booms, thus lowering the tail and raising the nose of the aircraft.

As the cockpit rose a foot or two into the air, the instructor, standing outside the aircraft, would tell the pilot to remember what the forward view looked like. To land the aircraft satisfactorily, it was necessary to put it in that attitude again if the pilot was to avoid either bumping the tail on the ground, or conversely, putting all three wheels on the ground together. This latter situation set up a violent shimmying of the nose wheel, in the manner of a tea trolley pushed too fast; very disconcerting to an inexperienced student!

The nose wheel seemed sometimes to have a mind of its own. Moving fast, it would shimmy; if taxied too slowly it wandered uncontrollably and the aircraft lurched all over the place. No wonder the pilot's notes for the type said, 'Taxi this aircraft boldly.'

A good-natured beast

In the air the Vampire was a good-natured beast and quite easy to fly. To those of us more experienced on piston-engined aircraft it had one trap for the unwary. If, with the engine throttled well back on an approach to land, it was necessary to abort the approach and climb away it was vital to open the throttle gently. Failure to do so produced an extraordinary rumbling and clatter from the engine without any noticeable increase in power.

The effects of lowering the flaps could surprise the uninitiated. De Havilland's tended in those days to design aircraft with the ability to lower large amounts of flap. In the case of the Vampire, the pilot could select 80 degrees of flap down; in other words the flaps went down almost at right angles to the wings. Inside the cockpit the effect of lowering so much flap was not unlike flying into a pat of butter. Selection of 'full flap' had to be followed with a brisk movement forwards on the stick to prevent a strong tendency for the nose to rise.

With the exception of these minor eccentricities, the Vampire provided a painless introduction to jet flight. As it was replaced in squadron service by more advanced types it found its way into various flying training units. Here, it served for several years as an advanced flying and

Introduced to the RAF in 1952, the Vampire T.11 became the first jet aircraft on which pilots qualified for their wings. More than 3,000 pilots gained their wings flying the T.11, which remained in RAF service until 1967. This early, heavy cockpit framed example, WZ551, is on strength with 229 OCU and remained in service with a variety of subsequent units until 1964. (Via Martyn Chorlton)

gunnery trainer, to good effect. As the airframe aged, some of the single-seat Vampires developed uncertain spinning characteristics. For a time, each aircraft had to be spun by a qualified instructor at least once a month to ensure that it was safe for students to fly.

In the training role, the Vampire FB.5 was joined by its two-seat descendant, the Vampire T.11. It was wide, with a bulbous nose to accommodate two pilots sitting side-by-side. The earliest version had a clamshell hood and no ejection seats. The hood was too small to allow both pilots to escape through it together so in the event of a mishap it was as well to have an understanding with your co-pilot about who was to bale out first. Pilots' notes merely said, 'The Captain should remain tightly strapped into his seat until the other occupant has cleared the aircraft.'

The next version had a magnificent one-piece hood, which allowed easy access and egress. It also possessed a neat central instrument panel instead of the two panels of the first version.

With healthy production and the fact that it served with 40 operational squadrons meant there was never any shortage of FB.5s for second-line Advanced Flying Schools, Flying Training Schools, Operational Conversion Units or Flying Refresher Schools. A 'pilot's aeroplane', the FB.5 was popular with all who flew it. (Via Martyn Chorlton)

No place for a tall man

The final version had a similar hood and was fitted with two ejection seats. Since the cockpit had not originally been designed to take these seats, the room left for the pilots was very restricted. The limited leg room meant that particularly long-legged student pilots risked losing their knee caps if they had to eject from the cockpit. Thigh lengths were measured and the taller chaps were trained on the Meteor T.7 in which, since it had no ejection seats, the problem ceased to exist.

The limited space in the Vampire T.11 meant that trying to sort out the four harness straps, two-leg restraint straps, oxygen lead, bail-out bottle connection, three dinghy connection and a radio lead could require a great deal of practice. Indeed, like a lot of aircraft, getting into the thing was the hardest part of flying it.

All marks of Vampire were delightful aerobatic machines, light and responsive. To those like me whose ability at aerobatic manoeuvres was more enthusiastic than skilled, it was a forgiving machine. To barrel roll it, with its delightfully light and responsive ailerons, was child's play. Being upside down over the Anglesey coast at the high point of a loop, with the sky beneath the floor and the little fields and the sea above my head, remains in my memory as part of my particular golden era.

A cold descent

As I drifted slowly down in my parachute after the collision I was in no mood to think about the finer points of aircraft handling. I was wearing only underwear, flying suit, shoes and socks, having lost my leather flying helmet as I baled out. The effects of cold (and it was well below zero at 18,000ft) were magnified by my state of shock. The rate of descent was almost imperceptible and for a while I worried in case I was not descending at all. I kept putting my hands into my mouth to try to keep them warm, afraid in case they would be too cold to release the parachute harness as I entered the water.

In the event, I could not release the harness. Seconds after the shock of dropping into the sea, I found myself on my back being towed by the parachute billowing across the water. This unpleasant process lasted for several minutes. Half drowned, I finally pulled off the shoulder straps of the parachute harness and climbed out of the leg straps.

With difficulty I inflated the dinghy and climbed in. It was a simple 'K' type—no hood or other protection, but to me it was a most welcome sight.

I had been seen entering the water by the pilot of another Vampire who reported my position to Air Traffic Control at Chivenor. For the next hour every aircraft in the area came to look at me; first a Tempest from the target-towing flight at Chivenor, then a civilian Auster en route to Lundy. Then, most terrifying of all, a Shackleton from St Mawgan dropped smoke floats to mark my position. The sight of the huge four-engined aircraft coming straight at me only a few feet above the water was almost more frightening than the accident itself. The starboard wing tip passed over my head accompanied by the noise of the four engines and the sight of a grinning co-pilot waving from the cockpit.

Soon afterwards my final visitor came to take me home—and incidentally gave me my first ride in a helicopter. I was rescued by a Sikorsky S.51 Dragonfly helicopter from Royal Naval Air Service (RNAS) Culdrose—my first, but certainly not my last, encounter with the Royal Navy.

Vampire T.11, WZ456, WZ470 and WZ459 of 208 Advanced Flying School (AFS) out of Merryfield, which was formed in November 1951 but redesignated as 10 Flying Training School (FTS) in June 1954. Of the three T.11s, WZ456 was abandoned near Newark in December 1957 while in service with the RAF College at Cranwell, WZ470 remained with 10 FTS until 1964, and WZ459 was written off at Church Fenton in 1966 when in service with 7 FTS. (*Aeroplane***)**

Chapter 7

Advanced Training on Sir Geoffrey's Blood-Sucking Mammal

Following the disbandment of 8 FTS on 19 March 1964, RAF Swinderby took on the role of recruit training and for many future airmen, their first sight of a station was this Vampire T.11 gate guard. XD506 never served at Swinderby until 1977 when the Vampire was mounted outside the main gate and would remain there until the station's closure in 1993. The aircraft is now under the care of the Jet Age Museum, Gloucester. (Martyn Chorlton)

Tony Haig-Thomas describes flight training in the Vampire.

RAF Swinderby
Our leave was soon over and my new car (a 1932 Morris 8 (restored!)) and I arrived at RAF Swinderby to re-join the rest of my course, or those that had not been 'scrubbed' on Jet Provosts. We were to fly Vampires with dual controls in the awful T.11 two-seat, side-by-side version, followed by solo flying in the heavenly single-seat FB.5, which was not only wonderful to fly but, best of all, had been retired from real fighter squadrons and some of them were still camouflaged. Swinderby was a hutted camp halfway between Newark and Lincoln. During the war it had been a heavy bomber station and later a conversion unit, but it had lots of hangars and, I guess, probably 80 Vampires, in total. The Vampire was powered by a Goblin engine with 3,500lbs of thrust; twice the power of our Viper-engined Jet Provosts. The Goblin engine's centrifugal compressor produced a wonderful wailing noise that, when I hear it today, takes me back in time just as much as Bill Haley's *Rock Around the Clock* does. I could never understand why the Goblin wailed so distinctively when the

very similar centrifugal compressors of the Derwents and Nenes made just a smooth whistling sound. We were introduced to our instructors; mine was 'Pete' Adair – 'Sir' to me – and he had been on a Meteor day-fighter squadron. There was a lot of one-upmanship among the students to have a fighter-pilot instructor and I felt even more superior to have one of my own.

The advanced flying course was largely a repeat of the Jet Provost course but with the addition of our first nibble at the effects of the speed of sound on subsonic aircraft. With its extra thrust, Sir Geoffrey's blood-sucking mammal could easily attain 35,000ft and, if one had time, 40,000ft could appear as another magical number on the altimeter. The Advanced Flying School training was again half ground school and half flying but, with our JP backgrounds, none of us had any trouble flying the aircraft although the air force still made us do nine or ten trips each before going solo.

The grim reaper strikes
So far during our training the grim reaper had stayed away from Hullavington but during our time at Swinderby he arrived and took two students and one instructor. The instructor was David Kirkup* who was posted to us from a Shackleton squadron; naturally no one wanted a heavy aircraft instructor and no one was to have him as it turned out. Our Flight Commander, Stan Sollitt, decided that the new instructor needed more formation flying before flying with us as an instructor and he was No.3 in a 'V' of Vampires. The formation climbed through cloud with an instructor leading, John Blount as No.2 on the right, and DK No.3 on the left. His formation flying was very rough and, descending back through cloud, his aircraft lost the formation, reappeared, banked straight at the leader followed by a rapid reversal away from him. When the formation broke through the cloud base there was a grim black pillar of smoke where DK's Vampire had crashed after failing to transition to instrument flight. No one seemed particularly concerned, but flying was cancelled for our course for one afternoon as the instructors all went to his funeral.

* Flt Lt David John Kirkup was killed in FB.5 VZ119 on 13 August 1957; aircraft crashed near Besthorpe, Notts.

EX31, High Speed Run
The Vampire was capable of climbing to height in a perfectly tolerable time and introduced us to the mysteries of 'the sound barrier' and why it was thus named. As subsonic aircraft approach Mach unity, shock waves form on lumps and bumps on the aircraft as localised airflow becomes temporarily supersonic and this leads to a breakdown of the airflow behind the shock wave. If a wave forms on one wing that wing will drop temporarily as it loses lift relative to the other; things get more exciting however if the shock wave destroys the airflow over the tailplane. An aircraft is stable in pitch because there is a permanent download on the tail – if, however, this download is suddenly reduced, the aircraft will pitch nose down very violently, the high Mach number will be maintained and pulling back on the stick will have very little effect if the elevators are blanketed behind the shock wave. The point of this elementary lesson in transonic aerodynamics is that there had been another fatal accident. A student pilot had died in his single-seat Vampire in a steep straight dive into the Lincolnshire countryside and it was thought that corrugations, which were certainly present on the tailplanes of all the single-seaters, might have been the source of multiple shock waves that triggered the dive and then, by leaving the elevators in disturbed airflow, prevented recovery. One of our instructors was Master Pilot Evans and he was given the task of doing a 'Mach run' in every single-seat Vampire at Swinderby to see if he could replicate the situation, but no problem was encountered. The whole hypothesis was improbable because if control is lost at high level extending the airbrakes and reducing power will cure the whole

unpleasantness as thicker air is encountered at around 15,000ft. Much the most likely cause was a lack of oxygen by the pilot, then known as anoxia, but now called hypoxia. It is easy now to criticise, but in 1957 it was only ten years since the legendary Yeager had become the first man to exceed Mach One in an aircraft and none of our instructors had flown supersonic. So, we climbed our Vampires and snaked and pitched and flicked and landed and wrote 'EX31 High Speed Run' in our logbooks. I loved that bit.

Sandys culls the air force
Shortly after the start of our flying at Swinderby the Minister of Defence, Duncan Sandys, stood up in the House of Commons to announce a new Defence White Paper. The principle part of this paper was to declare that manned fighter aircraft were a thing of the past and, from now on, air defence would be conducted by missiles. He was quite right about that but wrong in that he thought the missiles would be on the ground, where as, in fact, they would be air launched from air-superiority fighters. I failed to grasp the significance of this new defence policy and its impact on my life plan. Very shortly afterwards, however, it became clear as all the auxiliary Fighter Squadrons were disbanded together with most of the 2nd Tactical Air Force Squadrons in Germany, and a great swathe of the UK air defence squadrons in the home-based Fighter Command. Worst of all, the disastrous effect was felt immediately at Swinderby, as there were no postings to the Hunter Conversion units at all and the whole RAF was awash with fighter pilots who had nothing to do. We had six months' training left to get our wings and during that time there were no fighter postings and all graduating pilots were sent to Transport Command to fly four-engined Beverleys or Hastings with no opportunity to bag a couple of MIG-15s before breakfast. Things were bad.

Parade dodging
We all do things that we are, with hindsight, ashamed of and I am no exception. One day there was a full station parade - I overslept and consequently missed it. I had breakfast with one other student from another course in an otherwise empty mess and went down to 'the flights' full of trepidation. No one had missed me. There were two more parades scheduled so I did a tactical oversleep and still no one missed me. The parades were in anticipation of the Air Operations Centre's (AOC) annual inspection and there was a full dress rehearsal, one which even I thought that I should attend. When I arrived, I found that I was in 'battle dress', our everyday uniform, but everyone else was in 'best blue' No.1 Service Dress [SD]. There were, however, a few national service pilots who did not have a No.1 SD. First of all, there was a roll call (for the first time) and then, during the inspection, names were taken of the national service pilots who, because I was attired like them, erroneously included me and

Vampires of 8 FTS practice formation flying directly over their home station, RAF Swinderby, in 1956. (Crown copyright)

we were then excused all further parades. This did not make me very popular with the rest of my course as I wandered in on parade days having enjoyed a lengthy breakfast and the morning papers while they practised march-pasts and all the various drills that are laid on for visiting Air Marshals.

The other student pilot that I had breakfasted with on that first occasion with the genuine oversleep took off in Vampire FB.5, WA250** later that day and flew into a thunderstorm near Gainsborough. His aircraft broke up and an elderly couple, hearing a crash from upstairs, found a hole in their roof and his body in their bath. A little later the Mae West he had been wearing turned up, allocated to our squadron, complete with some bloodstains on it. Parsimony with the taxpayers' assets is to be commended but Stan Sollitt had it sent back to the safety equipment section together with some of the very succinct phraseology for which he was well known.

** This incident took place 13 May 1957, claiming the life of Acting Pilot Officer Thomas Patrick Cronin. His body was found by Mr and Mrs F P Coulson of 28 Claythorne Drive, Gainsborough.

High-level exercises
Our flying continued without incident. I had a problem with my instrument flying, or to be more specific with steep turns on limited panel, which involved three extra sorties; I loved the night flying and felt from my little cockpit with the glowing instruments and the quiet hum of the engine that I was alone in the centre of the universe. Perversely, as I was eventually to spend my air force career in the single-seat world, I was to do very little flying in the dark – had I done more, perhaps the novelty would have worn off; I doubt it. One high-level exercise that we flew could only be done in a Vampire and I know of no other jet that could fly it, a very high-level loop. The aim was to start at Mach 0.82, a whisper below the 0.84 at which the aircraft would, typically, start porpoising, and a height of 30,000ft. The aircraft was then inched into a climb, anything other than a very slight pitch input would cause it to enter a compressibility stall and start to flick. Very slowly, as the aircraft pitched up, increasing amounts of stick input could be applied until, if you were lucky, the little Vampire would fly over the top at close to 40,000ft with no airspeed, a ballistic trajectory, and full power from the Goblin producing around a quarter of its sea-level thrust. Any rough handling at any point during this manoeuvre would initiate a series of violent auto-rotational flicks; Jim Baldwin lost it on one flight and said that his aircraft had flicked up to 42,000ft before it fell off in a spin. Easy to see why this exercise was only flown dual.

I flew one sortie, which now being much older and wiser, I wish that I had not, but as a teenager one's judgment on such matters was never good. I had a session of solo aerobatics scheduled and the weather forecast was for a glorious summer day – which can happen in England from time to

A typical example of an 8 FTS Vampire FB.5, WA271 '89', which first joined 60 Squadron, and possibly saw action before being passed on to 4 Squadron and 7 FTS prior to arriving at Swinderby. The Vampire was not SOC until June 1960. (Via Martyn Chorlton)

time – so I decided that it was time for my parents and sibling sisters and brothers to see just what an ace their son and big brother had become after only a year's experience - not to mention the 150 hours total time in his logbook. I spent the night before with my maps and pilot's notes and found that I could take off from Lincoln, climb to 30,000ft, let down, give the family a 'beat up' and make it back to Swinderby via another 30,000ft climb. This is the classic and only way to fly a long-range strike in 1950s aircraft, although I did not know this at the time. The flight went as planned, the family lived on a little island near Harwich so there were no complaints and my sisters said that there was a horrid smell of paraffin after I had flown past. Clear evidence of success.

A dearth of Hunter postings

About two-thirds of the way through our advanced flying school course I became seriously worried about the complete block on the recruitment of fighter pilots; I had had a tremendous battle to get into the RAF with my appalling eyesight (6/9 6/12, with astigmatism, for those of a technical disposition) and now another fight was looming. It seemed impossible for the air force to block all recruitment forever, so I embarked on a sustained campaign on the simple principle of nothing ventured, nothing gained. One of the exercises that accompanied formation flying was 'tail chasing' where the two formating aircraft followed the leader around the sky holding a constant 200–300 yards behind solely by manoeuvring flight. If you were too close you allowed your aircraft to slide a little to the outside of a turn and vice versa; it could be very hard work, especially when dual, as the T.11 had ejection seats in a very small cockpit and the resultant upright posture is very uncomfortable when under sustained G. Whenever I flew dual-tail chase I used to fly as aggressively as possible and intersperse my grunts, greying vision and slight feelings of sickness with remarks such as 'Now we've got him, Sir, if only we had guns!' and other what now seem like rather immature comments. In short, I made it clear that air-combat manoeuvring was right up my street. My next opportunity came nearer the end of our course; I had committed some crime and been sentenced by Stan Sollitt to clean and tidy the Squadron Commander's office. I swept it out, emptied the ashtrays and wastepaper basket and then had a brainwave when I saw the blotting paper pad that was on all desks in those days, much as computers are now. I removed the top piece of much-used blotting paper and replaced it with a virgin white new piece, then, finding a red pen I wrote

With so many aircraft in the RAF inventory during the 1960s, attendance by home-based aircraft alone gave rise to a plethora of well-attended air displays and station open days. There was no shortage of 8 FTS aircraft available to attend air shows including Vampire T.11, XD435 at RAF Bentwaters in 1962. (Via Martyn Chorlton)

neatly in the top left-hand corner 'Memo – get Hunter posting for Plt Off Haig-Thomas'. I said nothing, he said nothing. Finally, just before the course ended, and following Stan Sollitt's discovery that I was wearing a very tasteful dark maroon pair of socks with my uniform, I was sentenced to write out 25 times why I was improperly dressed. I wrote neatly that, 'I was wearing red socks with my uniform as my black ones had been sent on to RAF Chivenor in anticipation of my Hunter conversion there.' Then I went to Station Head Quarters where a very helpful young WAAF 'Roneo'd' me 25 copies and the next day I placed these on Stan's desk. Again, nothing was said but no Hunter postings went to the course in front of us after graduation, so my prospects were not good.

Passing out
The day before our 'Wings' parade, I stood outside our flight offices with my instructor and Stan Sollitt when there was a mighty roar and a Gloster Javelin two-seat night fighter with a huge delta-shaped wing appeared from behind the hangars during an overshoot from a low approach. 'That will be Pete Poppy,' said Stan as the earth trembled with power. 'He used to instruct on our flight and he is just trying to piss me off.' I went weak in the knees with admiration, desire and jealousy.

Our passing-out parade came and went; it was my first touch from an Air Marshal as he pinned the wings on my breast. I stepped back and saluted after which we were meant to turn left and march off. I ended up left all right but through nerves, only after having turned right through 270 degrees, a manoeuvre that is not easy and certainly not in the drill books. Terror and awe in the presence of God had blown my mind but no one seemed to notice, to my great relief. We had a dining-out night for our course and I got drunk, not just tipsy but drunk; I never made the dinner and was helped back to my room by Andy Pryde and Graham Clements and then I was ill, very ill, all night. I was still ill the next morning and arrived very late at the Squadron where I was told never to let it happen again - and I never have.

Our course was sent en bloc to Valley on Anglesey in North Wales where we would await our postings and where we could stay in flying practice with the occasional Vampire flight. I was very proud to have my wings and very worried about my future.

The 5 FTS Vampire display team, made up of T.11s, XD450, XD506, XD545 and XD554, practise formation aerobatics not far from their home airfield at Oakington. All four aircraft survived their RAF flying careers without incident, all being SOC (Struck off Charge) between 1960 and 1967. (*Aeroplane*)

Chapter 8

Pioneering Jet-Powered Aerobat

A confident performer

Aerobatics have always played a prominent part in RAF pilot training. They are not performed merely to provide a spectacle for the public; they are an essential step in the making of a pilot, giving him complete confidence in himself and his aircraft. Formation aerobatics give him the added factor of confidence in his leader and other members of the team. Once the Vampire had entered service with the RAF in the late 1940s and formations had been tried, it soon became apparent that the type provided a good, stable and controllable mount for aerobatic flying.

In July 1947, 54 Squadron's commanding officer, Sqn Ldr Mike Lyne, formed what was known as the 'world's first jet-formation aerobatic team'. Operating from Odiham, it took three Vampires to the Grand International Aeronautical Gala at Evere, Belgium. In April 1948, the squadron team was disbanded and temporarily integrated into the Aerobatic Squadron (comprising 54, 72 and 247 squadrons), which was established from the RAF Odiham Vampire display teams formed for a goodwill tour of the USA and Canada. A record was achieved in July 1948 when the six Vampires of 54 Squadron became the first jet fighters to cross the Atlantic from west to east, followed by successful participation in exercises with the USAF and participating in air shows in the USA and Canada. During the same month, 72 Squadron's team, also from Odiham, performed in an air pageant at Gatwick, led by Sqn Ldr D Kingaby. This event was so popular that it was repeated the following year, renamed as The International Air Pageant and was attended by 90,000 spectators, who witnessed a programme that included another display by 72 Squadron's team of four Vampires.

One of several Flying Training Command units to put on a Vampire display was 4 FTS at Worksop. Four Vampire T.11s practice several thousand feet about the cloud-base, circa 1957. (*Aeroplane*)

Flt Lt 'Benny' Bennett leads 54 Squadron's five-strong Vampire display team in an impressive display at Farnborough in 1950. (*Aeroplane*)

Under the leadership of Flt Lt 'Benny' Bennett, 54 Squadron's team of five Vampires performed at the 1950 SBAC Show at Farnborough and also became the first jet aerobatic team to make smoke, trailing red, white and blue smoke across the Farnborough skies, which was witnessed by HM King George VI and HM the Queen, among 200,000 visitors to the show.

Teams in all theatres

Several other RAF Squadrons followed the lead in setting up their own aerobatic team on Vampires, especially in Germany during the early 1950s, where the 2nd Tactical Air Force was rapidly being expanded to meet the threat of the Cold War. No.3 Squadron at Gütersloh was the first German-based unit to form a team of Vampire FB.5s led by Flt Lt R Turner. Not to be outdone at Gütersloh, inter-squadron rivalry generated a second team at the base formed by 16 Squadron with Vampire FB.5s led by Sqn Ldr LH Lambert.

Further afield at Nicosia, Cyprus, three flying officers from 32 Squadron formed a trio of Vampire FB.3s, and in Malta, 73 Squadron formed a team of four FB.3s at Ta Kali led by Sqn Ldr RW Oxspring DFC. Even as far away as Singapore and Hong Kong, in the early 1950s, the RAF squadrons stationed there did not want to be left out. In Hong Kong, a team of three Vampire FB.9s was formed by 28 Squadron at Sek Kong, and in Singapore, Flt Lt K Cooke of 60 Squadron formed a team of four FB.9s at Tengah. There were now squadron teams in all operational theatres within the RAF.

By the mid-1950s, the popularity of RAF 'At Home' or family days had increased;

Another training unit to form display teams was 5 FTS. Here, in December 1955, the Vampire T.11 team, under the leadership of Flt Lt BW Seaman, is practising out of Oakington for the 1956 season. (*Aeroplane*)

70 RAF stations were open to the public in September 1953, putting on ground demonstrations and flying displays bringing in a total of 1,149,800 people. Squadrons were keen to form display teams to perform at these shows. Among the contributors for the 1954 At Home days were five teams of Vampires, together with teams of Meteors and Canberras, which were all shared between 56 RAF stations open to the public.

Teaching display flying from the start

The first permanent aerobatic display team at the RAF College, Cranwell, was formed in April 1956 with four Vampire FB.9s led by Flt Lt Colin Bidie. The previous year, No.5 Flying Training School (FTS) at Oakington formed two four-ship Vampire teams, one with T.11s led by Flt Lt BW Seaman and the other with FB.5s led by Flt Lt Colin Holman. By 1956, No.7 FTS at Valley and No.8 FTS at Swinderby had two teams each, with four Vampires, which performed at Battle of Britain At Home Displays. No.4 FTS, initially at Middleton St George and then at Worksop, also formed a Vampire team with FB.5s and 9s to display at several air shows. By 1959, the teams had acquired names to distinguish themselves from each other. Flt Lt George Black at No.1 FTS at Linton-on-Ouse, formed a four-ship Vampire T.11 team called the Linton Blacks. Meanwhile at No. 5 FTS at Oakington, the two four-ship Vampire teams were called The Hot Box and The Ice Box; presumably as both regularly flew in 'box' formation.

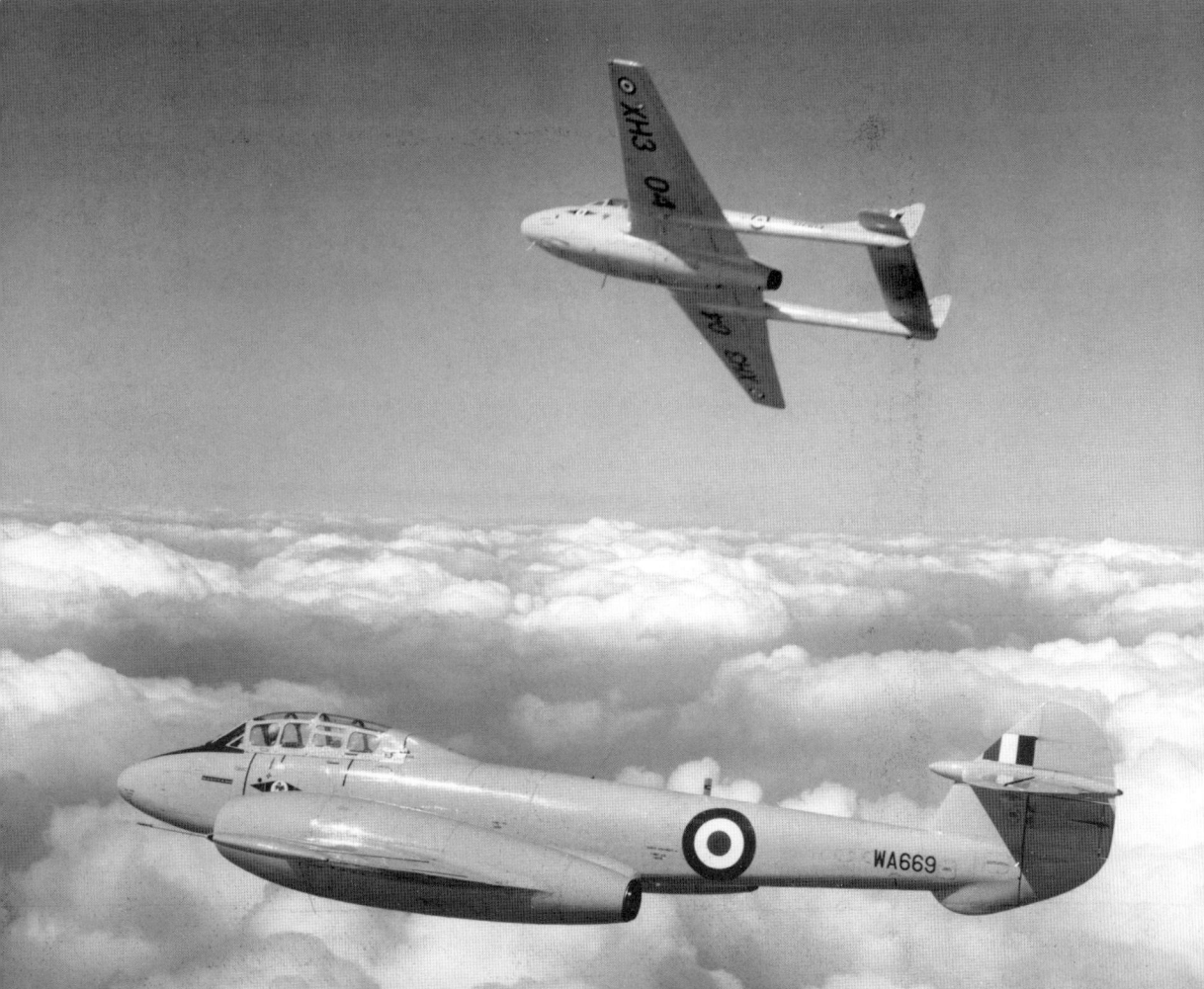

Popular performers on the British airshow circuit for 14 years, both aircraft of 'The Vintage Pair' (XK632 and XH304) were still used operationally by the CFS when not entertaining the public. (*Aeroplane*)

All these teams operated throughout the 1950s, but by the end of the decade, the Vampire fighters were being replaced by Hunters, while the Vampire T.11 was superseded by the Jet Provost. Therefore, the days of the fighter squadron Vampire display teams were coming to an end as the type was withdrawn from service. However, the Vampire T.11 teams from the FTSs and the RAF College continued into the early 1960s. It was not until 1960 that the Central Flying School (CFS) at Little Rissington formed a four-ship Vampire T.11 team, called Pelican Red. This was a 'warm-up' to the first of the Jet Provost T.3s that would replace the Vampires with the CFS and form the team called The Red Pelicans. During the early 1960s, the Vampire T.11s were rapidly being replaced by Jet Provosts throughout the training schools. The last Vampire T.11 aerobatic display team was operated by No.8 FTS at Swinderby in 1962. A three-ship display was led by Sqn Ldr NRC Price, taking in several of the Battle of Britain At Home displays, which had dwindled from 70 in 1953 to just 16 a decade later.

The long CFS swan-song

The Vampire's days as an aerobatic display mount were all but over in RAF service. However, the CFS was reluctant to let its last Vampire T.11 go and XK632 soldiered on until the early 1970s, forming a duo with Meteor T.7, WA669, called the CFS Historic Training Flight. In 1972, XK632 was retired and replaced by XH304; the duo being renamed The Vintage Pair. Both aircraft were repainted in light aircraft grey overall with yellow training bands, reminiscent of their 1950s livery and saw extensive exposure performing their aerobatic routine at air shows throughout the UK and Europe. They operated safely for 15 seasons until that fateful day of 25 May 1986, while performing at the USAF Mildenhall Air Fete, the Meteor collided with the Vampire's tail boom and both aircraft crashed.

Formed on 4 May 1949, the Royal Canadian Air Force's The Blue Devils, led by Flt Lt Don Laubman, were initially formed as a duo; this only lasted for a week before a third aircraft arrived. (Via Martyn Chorlton)

The Vampire T.11 had ejection seats and both occupants escaped, but the Meteor crew went down with their aircraft. That was the last time a Vampire T.11 flew in RAF service.

Performing in Canada

The first Commonwealth order was from the Royal Canadian Air Force (RCAF) in March 1947 for 85 F. Mk.3s to be built in Britain and assembled by de Havilland in Canada. Soon after delivery, a display team was formed at the CFS called The Vampire Flight, which was initially manned by two young fighter pilots, who had plenty of combat experience. Flt Lt 'Stocky' Edwards was in charge with Flt Lt 'Irish' Ireland his right-hand man. Together they became known as the 'Kerosene Kids' in reference to the new type of fuel used by the jets. Ireland was the first to fly 17014, undertaking a 30-minute trip on 4 February 1948. It was only a matter of weeks before word got around that this pair had formed a demo team and invites to air shows and events started coming in. The first demonstration was by Edwards on 15 March 1948, near Trenton, Ontario, in conjunction with an army display. 'Irish' Ireland relates how his demonstration days got started:

> As the first jet-propelled aircraft in Canadian service, the Vampire was much in demand for flying and static displays by both military and civilian organisations. Initially the flying displays consisted of single aircraft executing high- and low-speed flypasts, maximum rate turns, loops and rolls – all very impressive with the new sound and somewhat higher speeds of the jet aircraft. The demonstrations progressed into three and four-plane formations – the first three-plane display recorded was in Vampire 17013 during the opening of the World Trade Fair in Toronto on 29 May 1948. That was a straightforward flypast and was followed by another by the same three aircraft on the same day for the Ontario County Flying Club at Oshawa.
>
> Let not the wrong impression be given that these displays were a flagrant waste of flying hours. Most, if not all, of the simple flypasts were formation training flights for the numerous experienced pilots who were being 'converted' to jet aircraft operation. Scheduling of the flight and timing by the leader to appear at the right location at the appropriate time were critical features of the training flight. Our first international flying and static display was given at the Detroit International Air Show held at Romulus Airport on 26 and 27 June 1948. The aircraft were based at Selfridge Field, Michigan, and the entire affair was a great success

Following this introduction of the Vampire to display flying by the RCAF, the CFS was given the task of setting up the first air show jet team. Edwards would continue to do many solo aerobatic displays in the Vampire, but for Ireland a new development was about to take place. An increasing number of requests for the appearance of jet aircraft were coming in from the organisers of Air Force Days and local county fairs. These soon dictated more than an 'ad hoc' response, as and when aircraft were available. Accordingly, AVM EE Middleton, AOC Central Air Command, directed Wg Cdr FR 'Freddie' Sharp, OC CFS, to form an officially recognised aircraft display team. The appointed leader was Sqn Ldr Barry Barrett, an RAF exchange officer. A three-plane aerobatic routine was developed, with the first show being at Trenton in August 1948. This was followed by other shows in the region including one at Niagara Falls, New York. The following day, the team had their first accident, when Flt Lt Banner inexplicably crashed during the return cross-country flight from Niagara Falls. By October 1948, the display season was running down and some of the pilots were posted, many to the newly formed Air Defence Group (ADG) at St. Hubert, Quebec, which would continue the responsibility of aerobatic display flying over the coming years.

410 (Cougars) Squadron reformed in December 1948 with the Vampire F Mk3, but by 1951 the twin-boom fighter had already been replaced by the Canadair Sabre. (Via Martyn Chorlton)

At St. Hubert, 410(F) Squadron was reformed on 1 December 1948 alongside the formation of the ADG. On 4 May 1949, Flt Lt Don Laubman formed a duo of Vampires called The Blue Devils, which would continue to feed the public's interest in the new jet fighter. A week later, another Vampire, flown by Flt Lt Omer Levesque, joined the duo and The Blue Devils trained as a trio aerobatic team. Later a solo Vampire was added, flown by Flt Lt Joe Schultz, who would entertain the crowds with aerobatics, while the trio reformed, joining up in the box for the show's finale loop. The team's first show was at Rockcliffe, Ontario, on 11 June 1949, and was a great hit with the spectators, few of whom had seen formation aerobatics flown in jet aircraft at low level before.

The Blue Devils became the first officially authorised RCAF ADG aerobatic display team to perform at shows across Canada and the USA since the war. Shortly afterwards, a second solo Vampire was added to the team, piloted by Flt Lt Bill Tew. He would co-ordinate his simultaneous solo aerobatics with Joe Schultz. Later, a permanent fourth team member was added in the box flown by Fg Off Bill Bliss, which brought the team up to six aircraft.

The first show for The Blue Devils across the border in the USA came on 3–4 July 1949 when the team performed at Chicago's National Air Fair. By the end of the second day, 300,000 Americans had watched the pride of the RCAF perform. Then it was back to Canada and a show at Rockcliffe on 22 July. It wasn't long before a return visit to the USA was requested to attend a show in Michigan. However, during a team practice over the airfield of St. Hubert on 25 July, Sqn Ldr Bob Kipp was killed when his aircraft crashed during an inverted opposing pass with Joe Schultz. Nevertheless, the team participated at the Michigan Air Fair at Willow Run Airport, Detroit. Eleven successive shows followed in Canada at the Canadian National Exhibition, plus a two-day show at the National Air Races, Cleveland, Ohio, on 3–4 September 1949, making a total 26 displays in their first season.

The team continued in 1950 and 1951 with more shows in Canada and the USA, with some team member changes due to postings. The Blue Devils were finally disbanded in August 1951, to make way for teams of Sabres and other types coming into service.

Performing across the world

Meanwhile, across the other side of the world, the Australian government became the first overseas customer to purchase the Vampire trainer variant, when in 1951 it ordered 36 Vampire T.33s for the Royal

Australian Air Force (RAAF), followed by five T.34s for the Royal Australian Navy (RAN). A further order was placed for 68 T.35s and one T.34A to be built under licence by de Havilland Australia. The RAAF Vampires were based at Edinburgh, NSW, and at Pearce in Western Australia and with such a large fleet it was inevitable that an aerobatic team would emerge. This was The Telstars, formed at Edinburgh in 1966, later replaced by the Aermacchi MB-326Hs in 1969.

In Europe, the Italian Air Force's 4th Stormo formed a team of four Vampire FB.51s in 1950 named after the squadron insignia Cavallinio Rampante (Rampant Horses). Based at Grossetto, this was the first Italian aerobatic team to form since the end of the war. The team lasted for two years before converting on to the Sabre Mk 4 and reforming in 1956.

In 1958, the RNZAF created a Vampire team called the Jetobatics, which were formed for the air force's 21st Anniversary Airshow at Ohakea, with four Vampires from 75 Squadron. The team, led by Flt Lt John Clark Buckmaster, thrilled the crowds and captured the imagination of the public. After the Ohakea Airshow, the team toured New Zealand displaying at all the major airports.

The team was operational for one year before disbanding and it was not until November 1963 that another New Zealand Vampire team was seen, when Sqn Ldr Brian Stanley-Hunt of 75 Squadron formed an un-named five-ship Vampire team for Air Force Day at Ohakea on 22 February 1964. The aircraft were given a smoke-making capability and were retained for single shows in 1965 and 1966, increasing to seven shows in 1967. The Vampire display at Ohakea on 8 August 1967 resulted in a tragic crash. Fg Off Murray Whineray was killed in a landing accident after the display was complete.

Undaunted, the team continued to participate in six shows in 1968, and in 1969 the 75 Squadron team was finally given the name, the Yellowhammers, based on the squadron crest, and the aircraft were adorned with two crossed yellow hammers on the nose. Led by Sqn Ldr Ross Donaldson, the team's first show was at Wairoa on 26 January, followed by six more displays. The team was forced to disband at the end of May 1969 due to Sqn Ldr Donaldson being posted to the USN as an instructor on the A-4 Skyhawk, prior to the squadron re-equipping with the type.

A five-ship unnamed Vampire team formed to complete the 1969 season led by Sqn Ldr John Scrimshaw, the last Vampire display venue being at the RNZAC Pageant at Wanganui on 7 March 1970.

On the South African continent, the SAAF formed its first aerobatic team in 1953 and called it The Bumbling Bees, flying four T-6s. The team was drawn from the Flying School at Langebaanweg Air Base and was led by the Flying School's Commandant, Chris Prins. The team later transitioned to Vampire FB.9s from 1958 until 1967, when both the flying school and all the Vampire trainers were moved to Pietersburg Air Base.

Final fling

Back in the UK, although the RAF's last operational Vampire had been destroyed in a fatal accident in 1986, it was not the end of aerobatic display Vampire teams. Businessman Don Wood purchased several former Vampire T.55s and Venoms when the Swiss Air Force retired its aircraft and put them up for auction. A team of experienced civilian pilots was gathered to form the Source Classic Jet Flight comprising three Vampires and a Venom, or four Vampires, depending on availability. Operating from Bournemouth Airport, the team made its debut in 1993 and was seen at several air displays performing formation flypasts at venues across the south of England and Europe. Initially in the original Swiss Air Force colours, the aircraft were subsequently painted in several different schemes worn by Vampires and Venoms when in RAF and Royal Navy service. By the end of the decade, the team had disbanded; the aircraft were put up for sale in September 2007, ending the era of Vampire aerobatic display teams.

Three ex-Swiss Air Force Vampire T.55s in the foreground and Venoms beyond at Bournemouth in 1993. (Source Classic Jet Flight Via *Aeroplane*)

Sea Vampire F.20, VV138 of 702 Squadron rides the lift to the flight deck of HMS *Theseus* on 29 June 1950 during sea trials. Despite the trials being a success, the Sea Vampire was never adopted for carrier-borne operations but did serve the Royal Navy from shore bases until 1970. (*Aeroplane*)

Chapter 9

The Fleet Air Arm's Premier Jet Fighter

The Royal Navy leads the way

The Royal Navy had been very interested in the Vampire ever since the prototype arrived for assessment at the RAE at Farnborough in mid-1944. One of the RAE's tasks was to recommend the aircraft type that would be most suitable for deck-landing trials. The batch of early jets included in the selection were the E.28/39, Airacomet, Meteor and Vampire.

The second prototype Vampire, LZ551/G, had already undergone preliminary modifications with carrier operations in mind. These included larger flaps and dive brakes, which combined to lower the stalling speed and virtually eliminate float. A deck-landing assessment was undertaken at Hatfield by the Aerodynamic Flight's Commanding Officer, Lt Cdr Eric 'Winkle' Brown, who recommended that LZ551/G would be suitable for deck-landing trials once an arrestor hook was fitted.

A V-form arrestor hook was attached to LZ551/G at Christchurch and on return to Farnborough on 10 October 1945, proof testing began on the RAE's runway arrestor gear. Unfortunately, the Vampire's arrestor hook was not strong enough for the trial and the aircraft was returned to Christchurch for strengthening, and while there a 3,000lb Goblin 2 engine was also installed. Before returning to Farnborough, a teardrop canopy was fitted and the pitot tube was moved from the fin to the port wing, because of the high angles of attack envisaged during deck-landing trials.

By this time 'rumour control' was reporting that the United States Navy (USN) were preparing a P-80 Shooting Star for deck-landing trials, but the British were at a more advanced stage. Regardless, it

Lt Cdr Eric 'Winkle' Brown brings navalised Vampire prototype LZ551/G into land on HMS *Ocean* in December 1945. (*Aeroplane*)

De Havilland Sea Vampire F.20 VV149 during an air test out of Hatfield in November 1948. Delivered to 703 Squadron in May 1949, the jet went on to serve with 700, 702 and 771 squadrons until 1960. (*Aeroplane*)

was decided to waste no time and on 26 November 1945, LZ551/G was flown down to Ford by Lt Cdr Brown for Aerodrome Dummy Deck Landings (ADDLs) in readiness for the first landing on an aircraft carrier by a jet aircraft.

The day chosen for this historic event, 3 December, was far from perfect with a moderate swell and overcast sky. Off the Isle of Wight, HMS *Ocean,* under the command of Capt Caspar John, received a message from Lt Cdr Brown that he was about to proceed with a landing. Taking off from Ford at 11.05 hours, Lt Cdr Brown made a single low pass over HMS *Ocean* before entering a final turn at 100kts to land. He made the landing look easy as he picked up the No.1 arrestor wire, which brought the little jet to an abrupt halt. Not long after, Brown made history again by taking off, and following two further landings without trouble, the third saw the trailing edge of a flap hit the deck shearing off one of the hinged brackets. Later modified and reduced to give more clearance if landing with a wing down, the modified flaps were tested successfully again aboard HMS *Ocean* in early 1946.

Naval Test Squadron

Following the first, apparently successful deck-landing trials, the Ministry of Supply spent some time deciding whether or not to continue to the next stage of service acceptance. Many at the RAE thought that the Sea Vampire could only be flown onto a moving carrier's deck by exceptional pilots. These sentiments were endorsed by Lt Cdr Brown, but during a high-level meeting, attended by representatives from the RAE and the A&AEE at Boscombe Down, it was decided that the aircraft should be trialled by the Naval Test Squadron.

LZ551/G duly arrived at Boscombe Down in May 1946 to be trialled by 'C' Squadron of the Naval Test Squadron under the command of Cdr JA Levers. One of the test pilots was Lt SG Orr who served with 'C' Squadron from January 1946 to September 1948. Orr remembers the aircraft well:

> Sea Vampire LZ551 was sent to Boscombe Down in May 1946 for deck-landing trials to assess the feasibility of using jet aircraft on aircraft carriers. This aircraft had been at RAE Farnborough the

Lt Cdr Brown takes off from the deck of HMS *Ocean* in LZ551/G during the highly successfully trials in early 1946, after the flaps were modified. (*Aeroplane*)

previous year and had carried out the first-ever landing by a jet aircraft on a carrier. However, the results from these trials were inconclusive as to whether there were any fundamental problems, so the Admiralty decided to ask for a second opinion from the pilots at A&AEE. Three naval pilots, including myself, carried out simulated deck-landing trials on a marked area of the Boscombe runway, using various types of approach to establish the best procedure, and this was followed by full deck-landing trials on HMS *Triumph* in June 1946. It soon became evident that a jet aircraft with a tricycle undercarriage had distinct advantages over many piston-engined aircraft as, for the first time, the pilot had a completely unobstructed view of the deck area on the final approach. Secondly, with a tricycle undercarriage, it was possible to ease the stick forward on crossing the round down without reducing engine RPM. This resulted in a positive deck contact and, should the hook fail to engage an arrester cable, the RPM were high enough to ensure an immediate engine response for going round again. This procedure would not have been practical with the tail-wheel type undercarriage, as the result would have been to bounce over all the arrester wires. Recommendations were therefore made to the Admiralty to proceed with the development of jet-powered naval aircraft, as there were no serious problems with deck operation.

Selection for carrier operations

Further trials with LZ551/G were carried out on board HMS *Ocean* by the A&AEE, which highlighted a few more areas in need of modification. These included a longer-stroke undercarriage, improved throttle response and a connection between the flaps and the throttle to provide better lift control.

Designated as the Sea Vampire F.10, LZ551/G, it was then passed on to 778 Squadron at Ford, the Service Trials and Carrier Trials Unit, in July 1946, for further evaluation, until the aircraft was damaged aboard HMS *Illustrious*. By this time, the Admiralty had already decided that the Sea Vampire would not be suitable for carrier operations because of the engine's slow throttle response

Sea Vampire F.20s of 702 Squadron on board HMS *Theseus* on 29 June 1950, during sea trials. Under the command of Lt ABB Clark, VV150, being manhandled off the carrier's lift in the foreground, was one of six Sea Vampire F.20s allocated to the Naval Jet Evaluation and Training Unit. (*Aeroplane*)

and the aircraft's limited range. However, the excellent maintenance record of the aircraft and low-operating costs would make the little fighter ideal for introducing the FAA to jet operations.

As a result, specification 45/46P (later complemented by 46/46P) was issued on 14 January 1947 to cover the design of the Sea Vampire, which would be built at Preston by English Electric. Improvements to the production aircraft included an improved undercarriage, bigger dive brakes and landing flaps, upgraded arrestor hook and a new VHF radio set.

The Sea Vampire F.20

On 21 March 1947, an order for 30 Sea Vampire F.20s, serialled VV136–165, was placed under Contract No.6/Acft/1053/CB.7(a). By January 1948, this order had been reduced to 18 aircraft, serialled VV136–153.

Built at Preston, all 18 Vampire FB.5s were flown to Hatfield for conversion to Sea Vampire F.20 standard between November 1947 and January 1948. The prototype F.20 was converted from Vampire F.3, VF317, which arrived at Hatfield on 1 May 1947. Work involved the fitment of a V-frame arrestor hook, which was stored in a small housing above the tail pipe when not deployed. A substantial longer-stroke undercarriage was fitted capable of absorbing a landing of up to 16ft/sec. The wings were clipped as per the FB.5, and accelerated take-off hooks were mounted under each wing. The air brakes were increased by 36 per cent over the standard Vampire, as were the split trailing-edge flaps, which were 31 per cent larger.

The Sea Vampire F.20 made its service debut with 806 Squadron at RNAS Sydenham when VF315 was delivered by John Cunningham on 20 May 1948. The unit then embarked on HMCS *Magnificent* for a three-month tour of Canada and the USA, where the aircraft flew for 40 flying hours and covered 4,000 miles. While service trials continued with the A&AEE, carrier trials were performed by 703 Squadron, Naval Air-Sea Development Unit/Service Trials Unit (NASWDU/STU) from October 1948, operating from Tangmere on shore and HMS *Illustrious* at sea. Flying VV137 and VV138, 703 Squadron carried out approximately 60 landings on *Illustrious* with the two Sea Vampires without incident.

Six Sea Vampire F.20s were allocated to the reformed 702 Squadron at Culdrose in April 1949. Under the command of Lt ABB Clark, the unit was designated as the Naval Jet Evaluation and Training Unit, initially using HMS *Implacable* for shipboard trials. Further trials were conducted on HMS *Theseus* and on 19 June 1950, Lt Clark, in VV138, undertook the first-ever landing on an aircraft carrier at night.

Considering how few F.20s were built, the aircraft managed to serve with 700, 728, 759, 764 and 771 squadrons. The type remained in service until April 1956 when the last examples were retired by 700 Squadron at Ford.

A dramatic image of Lt Cdr Brown in Vampire F.1, TG286 moments before the aircraft pitched heavily during flexible deck trials at Jersey Brow, Farnborough, on 29 December 1947. Even though the cockpit structure was split and the aircraft written off, Lt Cdr Brown walked away unharmed. (*Aeroplane*)

Flexible deck F.21s

The idea of improving the performance of the Vampire, by dispensing with an undercarriage and recovering the aircraft by landing on a mattress-type runway, had been first trialled with Vampire F.1, TG426 in December 1947 at Jersey Brow, Farnborough. The first such landing, flown by Lt Cdr Brown, did not go well and the aircraft was written off in the subsequent crash landing. Undeterred, a second F.1, TG238 was trialled successfully and from June 1948 a fully navalised aircraft, designated the Sea Vampire F.21, joined the experiment.

Only six aircraft, VG701, VT795 and VT802–805 were converted to F.21 at Hatfield to specification N.18/47 titled Design of Vampire for Flexible Deck Operation. Modifications included a reinforced lower fuselage pod and jet pipe fairing, reduced fuel capacity from 330-gallons to 203-gallons, and installation of an accelerometer. The arrestor hook was electrically lowered, rather than relying on gravity and within the hook itself, a trigger was fitted, which made sure that once it had grasped the wire both the flaps and dive breaks automatically closed to avoid damaging them.

The first of two pre-production Vampire trainers supplied to the Royal Navy for assessment in January 1952 was WW458. The aircraft was also trialled by 759 Squadron at RNAS Culdrose and 781 Squadron at Lee-on-Solent before being withdrawn in 1954 for instructional airframe duties. (Via Author)

By early November 1948, following successful trials at Jersey Brow, the light fleet carrier HMS *Warrior* was prepared for flexible deck trials. On 4 November, TG286 made the first landing followed by VT795, VT803 and VT805. Between November 1948 and May 1949 at least 200 successful landings were made on *Warrior* by VG701, VT803 and VT805 virtually free of any major incident. The whole concept eventually moved on to the Hawker Sea Hawk, one of which was trialled in 1953 by which time defence cuts brought the whole idea to a close.

A jet trainer for the Navy

Following the entry into service of the RAF's Vampire T.11, the Royal Navy was keen to gain its own jet trainer. All flying training up to 'wings' standard was provided by the RAF for FAA pilots, but a jet trainer in Royal Navy service would be employed for jet conversion, operational flying and weapons training and ADDL training.

In 1952, two Vampire T.11s, WW458 and WW461, were evaluated by the Royal Navy, which after several recommendations placed an order under specification T.111 P.2 in April 1952. To be built at Christchurch, the Navy's requirements included the installation of a TR.1936 VHF radio, A.1271 and ZBX radio-beacon equipment, a signal discharger operable by the pilot and anti-G fitments. There was no requirement for an arrestor hook or folding wings as the trainer would never be operated on an aircraft carrier.

On 10 February 1952, Contract No. 6/Acft/7704/CB.7(a) was issued for 53 Sea Vampire trainers serialled XA100–131 and XA152–172. Allocated the designation T.22, the first production aircraft, XA100 was ready in April 1953 but was retained by de Havilland for company trials and then allocated to the A&AEE in February 1954.

The Sea Vampire T.22 first arrived at Stretton on 18 September 1953, and after being prepared for service was allocated to 781 Squadron at Lee-on-Solent from October 1953. 736 Squadron at Lossiemouth and 759 Squadron at Culdrose followed in November 1953, both units conducting operational conversion courses for pilots posted to front-line units.

The first Sea Vampires built were produced to the same early RAF standard complete with a framed canopy and no ejection seats. Those T.22s already in service were steadily returned to Chester for modification between 1956 and 1957, the work including the fitment of an improved frameless canopy and a pair of ejection seats.

An early example of a Sea Vampire T.22, which has been brought up to later standard is XA109 '990/CU' serving with the Culdrose Station Flight during the early 1960s. This aircraft was saved from the axe and/or fire dump and today can be seen at the excellent National Museum of Flight at East Fortune, Scotland. (Via Martyn Chorlton)

A second order for 20 Sea Vampire T.22s was placed to Contract No. 5/Acft/10521/CB.7(a) on 24 June 1954. Serialled XG742–748 and XG765–777, the first aircraft were delivered to Stretton on 3 November 1954 and the last, delivered direct to Lossiemouth, on 25 May 1955.

The T.22 saw extensive service in the FAA with the following squadrons – 700, 700X (Trials Unit), 702, 718, 727, 728 (Fleet Requirements), 750 (Royal Navy Observer School), 764, 766, 802, 806, 808 (RAN), 809, 831 (Electronic Warfare Unit), 890, 891, 892, 893, 1831 and 1832 until May 1965. Several Sea Vampire T.22s lingered on after their squadron service had ended as 'hacks' or 'Admiral's barges', flown by the Flag Officer Flying Training and other senior officers. The last T.22 in FAA service was XA129, which was operated by the Air Direction School at Yeovilton until July 1970.

Above right: Sea Vampire T.22s undergoing modification, including a frameless canopy and ejection seats, at Chester in late 1956. (Via *Aeroplane*)

Below: Federal Works (F+W)-built Vampire FB.6s, J-1170 and J-1192, two of 100 built under licence between 1950 and 1952. The duo is pictured in the early 1980s when several surviving FB.6s were updated with new UHF radio equipment which was fitted into a Venom-type upturned nose. (Via Martyn Chorlton)

Chapter 10
Service in the World's Air Forces

Above left: Keen to re-equip its air force as quickly as possible with jet-powered aircraft, the Swedish Air Force was the first of many de Havilland overseas' customers. The first two aircraft, a pair of F.1s (redesignated as J.28As), can be seen at Hatfield in June 1946. (*Aeroplane*)

Above right: The first Vampire T.33 to enter RAAF service was A79-801 on 16 October 1952, which went on to serve with 2 OCU at Williamtown, New South Wales. (Via Martyn Chorlton)

AUSTRALIA
Royal Australian Air Force (RAAF)
21 (City of Melbourne) Sqn FB.5, F.30 and T.35 at Laverton; **22 Sqn**; **23 (City of Brisbane) Sqn** at Amberley; **25 (City of Perth) Sqn** F.30, FB.31 and T.35 at Pearce; **75 Sqn** FB.9 and F.30 at Williamtown; **76 Sqn** FB.9, T.33 and T.35A at Williamtown; **1 AFTS** T.35 at Pearce; **2 OCU** F.2, F.30, FB.31, T.33 and T.35A at Williamtown; **2 (F)OTU** T.35 at Williamtown; **5 OTU*** T.35 at Williamtown; **CFS** T.35 at East Sale; and **ARDU** FB.32 and T.35 at Laverton.
*Final Vampire sortie flown by **5 OTU** on 18 September 1970

Royal Australian Navy (RAN)
723 Sqn T.34 (Jun 1954–Oct 1956) at Nowra; **724 Sqn** T.22 (Jun 1955–70) and T.34A** (Jun 1957–Jan 1966) at Nowra.

** Final flight of an RAN Vampire on 5 October 1970.

AUSTRIA
Austrian Air Force
T.11 and T.55 (1956–Apr 1972) at Zeltweg, Wien-Aspern and Graz-Thalerhof.

BURMA
Myanmar/Burmese Air Force
T.55 (Dec 1954–late 1950s) at Mingaladon.

CANADA
Royal Canadian Air Force (RCAF)
400 (City of Toronto) Sqn F.3 (Mar 1948–Oct 1956) at Downsview; **401 (City of Westmount) Sqn** F.3 (Mar 1948–Oct 1956) at St Hubert; **402 (City of Winnipeg) Sqn** F.3 (Mar 1948–Oct 1956) at Stevenson; **410 (Cougar) Sqn** F.3 (Jan 1949–1951) at St Hubert; **411 (County of York) Sqn** F.3 (Mar 1948–Oct 1956); **421 Sqn** F.3 at Odiham; **438 (City of Montreal) Sqn** F.3 (Mar 1948–Oct 1956); **442 (City of Vancouver) Sqn** F.3 (Mar 1948–Oct 1956); **1(F) OTU** F.3 (Aug 1948–1952) at St Hubert and Chatham; **CFS** F.3 (from Jan 1948) at Trenton; **Experimental and Proving Establishment (renamed Central Experimental Proving Establishment)** F.3 at Rockcliffe and Namao; **Flying Instructors School** F.3 at Trenton; and the **Winter Experimental Establishment** F.1 at Edmonton.

CEYLON
Royal Ceylon Air Force
T.55 (1954). Five aircraft delivered but returned in favour of the Boulton Paul Balliol.

CHILE
Fuerza Aérea de Chile/Chilean Air Force: *4 Grupo* T.11/22 (1973–80) at Los Condores; **7 Grupo** T.11/22 and T.55 (Apr 1954–62) at Los Cerrilos and **8 Grupo** T-55 (1958–71; T.11 (1972–80) and Sea Vampire T.22 (1972–80) at Cerro Moreno.

DOMINICAN REPUBLIC
Fuerza Aérea de Republica Dominicana/Dominican Republic Air Force
Escuadron de Caza-Bombardero and **Escuadron de Caza 'Ramfix'** (later combined into the **Escuadron de Combate)** F.1 (J.28A), 1956–74 and FB.50 (J.28B) (1957–74) at San Isdrio.

In 1955, the Swedish company Henry Wallenberg brokered a deal to sell 25 ex-Swedish Air Force J.28As to the Dominican Republic. Some of the Vampires, serialled 2701–2725, are on the line at San Isdrio in 1956 while serving with Escuadron de Caza-Bombardero. (Via Martyn Chorlton)

EGYPT
Egyptian Air Force
2 Sqn FB.52 and T.55 (1952–56) at Kabrit; **30 Sqn** FB.52 (1952–56) to Almaza; **31 Sqn** FB.52 (1955–56) at Kabrit and **40 Sqn** FB.52 and T.55 and the **Fighter Training Unit** FB.5, FB.52 and T.55 (1955–56) at Almaza.

FINLAND
Ilmavoimat/Finnish Air Force
HavLv 11 FB.52 and T.55 (Jan 1953–56) at Pori; **LavLv 13** (FB.52 and T.55); **HavLv 21, 1 Lennosta** (renamed Hameen Lennosto) FB.52 and T.55 (1956–15 Jul 1965) at Jyvaskyla; **HavLv 31** FB.52 at Utti.

INDIA
Indian Air Force
7 Sqn FB.52 (Nov 1948–Jan 1958) at Palam; **10 Sqn** FB.52 and NF.54 (1954 to late 1960s) at Palam; **24 Sqn** FB.52 (Aug 1965–late 1960s); **37 Sqn** NF.54 (1957–62) at Poona; **45 Sqn***** FB.52 (Aug 1965–70); **101 Sqn** PR.55 (Oct 1954–68) at Adampur; **108 Sqn** PR.55 (Nov 1959–late 1960s); FB.52 (Aug 1965–late 1960s) at Halwara; **121 Sqn** FB.52 (Aug 1965–late 1960s); **220 Sqn***** FB.52 (Aug 1965–69); **221 Sqn** FB.52 (Aug 1965–late 1960s); **Aircraft Testing Unit** FB.52; **Armament and Aircraft Testing Unit** FB.52 at Cawnpore; **Armament Training Wing** T.11 and T.55 (until 1975) at Jamnager; **Fighter Training Wing** FB.52, T.11 and T.55 (until 1975) at Hakimpet; **Flying Instructors School** F.52, T.11 and T.55 (until 1975) at Tambaran.

***45 and 220 squadrons operated as one during the war against Pakistan in September 1965.

Indian Navy
FB.52 and T.55 (1958–mid-1960s); **300 Sqn** Sea Vampire T.22.

INDONESIA
Tentara Nasional Indonesia Angkatan Udara/Indonesian Air Force
T.55 (Feb 1956–58). All eight aircraft sold to India.

Indonesia ordered eight Vampire T.55s (serialled J-701–708) in 1955; the first of them being accepted at Hatfield in September 1955. Their service was short, and by the late 1950s all of them were serving with the Indian Air Force. (Via Martyn Chorlton)

IRAQ
Royal Iraqi Air Force
5 Sqn FB.52 (May 1953–early 1960s); T.55 (Dec 1953–early 1960s) at El-Rashid and Habbaniya.

IRELAND
Irish Air Corps
1 Sqn T.55 (May 1956–1975) at Baldonnell.

ITALY
Aeronautica Militare/Italian Air Force
1 Zona Area FB.52A at Milan/Brescia; **Stormo** FB.52A at Bergamo; **3 Group Flight School (renamed All-Weather Fighter School – Scuola Caccia Ogni Tempo)** NF.54 (1953–Oct 1959) at Foggia/Amendola; **3 Group Training School (later 7 Group Training School)** FB.52A; at Foggia/Amendola; **3 Zona Area** FB.5A at Rome/Ciampino; **4a Aerobrigata** FB.52A; **4 Stormo Cassia** FB.52A at Napoli/Capodichino; **4 Zona Area** FB.52A at Foggia/Amendola; **79 and 81 Squadriglia, 6 Gruppo** FB.52; **Aeronautica Militare Italiana** FB.5; **Reparto Sperimentale Volo** NF.54 (from 1959) at Practica di Mare; **Scuola Turbogetti** NF.54; **Jet Flying School** FB.5 at Foggia/Amendola; **Squadriglia Volo Senza Visibilita of 4 Stormo** NF.54 at Napoli/Capdichino.

This aircraft, Vampire T.55 '333', together with six Vampire FB.52s, formed the Iraqi Air Force's first jet-fighter unit, 5 Squadron based at El-Rashid, near Baghdad. (*Aeroplane*)

JAPAN
Japan Air Self Defence Force: T.55 (1956) at Hamamatsu.

JORDON
Royal Jordanian Air Force
1 Sqn FB.9, FB.52 (ex-Egypt) and T.11 (1955–58 and again in 1962) at Amman; **2 Sqn** FB.9, FB.52 (1958–67).

KATANGA
Katangese Air Force T.11 (1961) at Kowezi.

LEBANON
Lebanese Air Force
Pursuit Bomber Squadron (renamed) 1 Sqn FB.52 (Oct 1953–64); T.55 (Aug 1953–64); FB.9 (1958–64) at Rayak and Khaldeh; Vampire not fully retired until September 1974.

MEXICO
Fuerza Aérea de Mexicana/Mexican Air Force
Escuadron Aereo de Palea 200 F.3 and T.11 (1962–70) at Aeropuerto International and Base Aerea Militar No.1, Santa Lucia; **Air College** instructional airframes at Zapopan.

NEW ZEALAND
Royal New Zealand Air Force
14 Sqn FB.53 (1951–59 and 1970–72; T.11 (1952–59 and 1970–72); and FB.9 (1952–59) at Ohakea; **75 Sqn** FB.5 (1952–70); T.11 (1952–70) at Ohakea; **Fighter Operational Conversion Flight (part of 75 Sqn)** FB.5 and T.11 (1954–72) at Ohakea.

NORWAY
Royal Norwegian Air Force
331 Skv F.3 (1949) at Gardermoen; **336 Skv** FB.52 (1950–Feb 1953) at Gardermoen; **337 Skv** FB.52 (1950–55); T.55 (1952–55) at Gardermoen; **339 Skv** FB.52 (1950–55) at Gadermoen; **Jet Training Wing** (T.55, Jul 1952–55) at Sola.

PORTUGAL
Força Aérea Portuguesa/Portuguese Air Force
Evaluation T.55 (Oct 1952–53) at Pora; **Jet Training Squadron** T.55 (1953–61) at BA 1, Sintra.

RHODESIA/ZIMBABWE
Royal Rhodesian and Zimbabwe Air Force (from 1979)
1(F) Sqn FB.9 (1956– 63) at New Sarum; **2(F) Sqn** FB.9 (Oct 1956–early 1980s) at New Sarum; **4 (Training) Sqn** FB.9 and T.11 (Sep 1958–early 1970s); T.55 and FB.52s (from 1969–early 1970s) at Thornhill.

SAUDI ARABIA
Royal Saudi Air Force
5 Sqn FB.52 (from Egypt) (Jul 1957–58) at Jeddah.

SOUTH AFRICA
South African Air Force
1 (City of Pretoria) Sqn FB.5 (1951–56) at Waterkloof and Swartkop; **2 (Cheetah) Squadron** FB.9 (1953–56); **Air Operational School (renamed Advanced Flying School)** FB.5 and T.55 (mid 1952–66) at Langebaanweg and Pietersburg.

SWEDEN
Flygvapnet/Royal Swedish Air Force
F3 J.28A (1950–53) at Malmslatt; **F4** J.28B (1952–57) at Froson; **F5** FB.50 (J.28B) and T.11 (Sk.28B and C) (1953–68) at Lungbyhed; **F8** J.28B (May 1949–53 and 1954–65) at Barkarby; **F9** J.28B (Jun 1949–52) at Gothenburg; **F10** J.28B (1951–53); **F11** J.28B (1953–55) at Nykoping; **F13** J.28A (Jun 1946–52) at Norrkoping; **F14** FB.50 (A.28B) (1953–57) at Halmstad; **F15** FB.50 (J.28B) (1952–56) at Soderhamn; **F18** J.28 (1950–57) at Tullinge; **F20** J.28A (1953–56) at Uppsala; **F21** J.28B (1954–55) at Lulea; the **Central Flying School** Sk28B (1956–67); J28C (1953–68) at Lungbyhed.

SWITZERLAND
Flugwaffe/Swiss Air Force
Fl.St. 7 FB.6 (1950–73) at Interlaken; **Fl.St.9** FB.6 (1950–67) at Meiringen; **Pilotenschule 1** T.55 (Jan 1956– 80s) at Sion/Emmen; **Zielfliegerkorps 5** FB.6 (1978–90) at Sion.

Service in the World's Air Forces

The first of two Hatfield-built Vampire NF.54s, 3-167 'MM6016' was delivered to 3 Group Flight School at Foggia/Amendola on 4 June 1951. The remaining 14 were built at Chester and delivered/ferried by Italian pilots between October 1952 and March 1953. (Via Martyn Chorlton)

SYRIA
Syrian Air Force
FB.52 (Oct 1956 to early 1960s) and T.11 (embargoed in 1956).

VENEZUALA
Fuerza Aérea Venezolana/Venezuelan Air Force
Escuadron de Caza 35 FB.52 (Dec 1952–72); and T.55 at Boca de Rio; **El Liberator and Grupo Aereo de Caza 12 (comprising Esc. De Caza 34** Venom, **Caza 35** FB.52 (1961–72) and **Caza 36** F-86 at Landaeta Gil and El Liberator.

Sea Venom NF.20, WK385, and Vampire T.11, WZ459 tail chase for the camera, while en route to SBAC at Farnborough in 1952. (*Aeroplane*)

Chapter 11
The Auxilliaries

The pilots and ground crew of 501 (County of Gloucester) Squadron scramble to their Vampire F.1s during exercise foil, a huge air-defence exercise, which involved all of the Royal Auxiliary Air Force (RAuxAF) Vampire squadrons. (*Aeroplane*)

Thirteen squadrons of the Royal Auxiliary Air Force operated the Vampire from 1948 through to its disbandment in 1957.

605 Squadron

There had always been good-natured competition between all 21 of the auxiliary squadrons, ever since the first, 602 (City of Glasgow), was formed at Renfrew on 12 September 1925. All had been disbanded by September 1945 only to be reformed the following year in a new post-war, Royal Auxiliary Air Force, to be equipped with either the Spitfire or Mosquito. However, it was clear that the first jets, the Meteor and the Vampire, were close to being available; 616 (South Yorkshire) had already bagged the Meteor at the end of World War Two while the Vampire was still for the taking.

The prize of becoming the first auxiliary unit to re-equip with the Vampire was won by 605 (County of Warwick) Squadron, which received its first F.1 at Honiley in July 1948, in place of the Mosquito NF.30 and T.3. Re-equipping of the Mosquito had been painfully slow and after reforming in May 1946, the unit was not declared operational on the type until August 1947. However, by the following summer, during a detachment to Tangmere, 605 Squadron was re-equipped with the Vampire and spirits were high again. By 1949, the first of many annual camps to Sylt in Germany was successfully undertaken, the squadron making full use of the neighbouring range for air-to-air and air-to-ground weapons training.

Only a single Vampire F.3 was added in February 1950, while a major change came in April 1951 when the unit's trusty F.1s were relinquished for the much improved FB.5. Up to this time, the

Vampire FB.5, VZ831 '47', of 602 (City of Glasgow) Squadron departing an air display circa 1952. After converting from the Spitfire F.22 in January 1951, 602 Squadron saw out its days with the Vampire FB.5 up to its disbandment at Abbotsinch on 10 March 1957. (*Aeroplane*)

Vampire F.1s of 605 (County of Warwick) sporting the three-letter reserve code of which the 'RA' part was applicable to all auxiliary squadrons. Later, when the squadrons were incorporated into Fighter Command, the traditional two letter code system was reintroduced. (*Aeroplane*)

squadron's safety record had been impeccable but the first loss came on 5 August 1951 when WA363 force landed one and a half miles southwest of Frampton-on-Seven, following engine problems; the pilot escaped unhurt. A second FB.5 was written off before the year was out, on 3 November, when the engine of WA364 failed on take-off at Honiley and belly landed back onto the runway; again without injury to the pilot.

1952 was a memorable year for the unit because it was given the 'Freedom of Entry' to the city of Coventry, which involved a big parade on the ground and large flypast in the air. As well as the aircraft of 605 Squadron, the Vampires of 613 (City of Manchester) and the Meteors of 504 (County of Nottingham) took part in an impressive flypast.

605 Squadron's only post-war fatality occurred on 27 November 1955 when Fg Off Grahame Otto Hauser was killed in the circuit at Honiley. His aircraft, WA457, suffered an engine failure and while attempting to force land, the Vampire struck trees and burst into flames one mile south of the airfield. The only other incident involved another belly landing on the runway on 16 September 1956 when the engine of VV479 cut on take-off. By the following year, the axe fell for the RAuxAF, when on 10 March 1957, 605 (County of Warwick) Squadron was disbanded.

The old and the new of 601 (County of London) Squadron in November 1949, at North Weald, after the unit received its first Vampire F.3s. The Squadron replaced the Spitfire LF.16E, two of which can be seen parked opposite. (*Aeroplane*)

Chapter 12
The 'Thin-Wing' Vampire

The prototype de Havilland DH.112 Venom, VV612, originally designated the Vampire F.8 (or FB.8) taking off from Farnborough during the annual SBAC in July 1950. (*Aeroplane*)

Developing the Vampire

By the end of the World War Two, the staff at de Havilland were rounding off the development of the de Havilland Goblin-powered DH.100 Vampire F.1 and turned their attention to later versions. The emergence of more powerful jet engines, such as the Rolls-Royce Nene, saw the arrival of the Vampire F.2, while the F.8 was being nurtured on the drawing board to accommodate the de Havilland Halford H.2 engine, later renamed the Ghost. The new engine fitted into the Vampire's airframe with little trouble and was only distinguishable by slightly large intakes over the earlier Goblin machines.

There was little or no interest in the new higher performance Vampire from the Ministry of Supply (MoS) but de Havilland ploughed on regardless and fitted a Ghost into an early mark for trials in connection with the forthcoming Comet airliner. This aircraft was in the air by May 1947. On 23 March 1945, John Cunningham set a new world record in the modified Vampire, reaching 59,446ft (18,119m). In June 1948, the MoS acknowledged the progress being made by de Havilland and agreed to fund a single prototype, designated the DH.112.

Double the thrust and reduce the wing

The Ghost engine, with 4,850lbs of thrust was more than twice as powerful as the first-generation Goblin and to take advantage of this, all attention was turned to improving the wing. Despite the advances achieved by the swept-wing DH.108, it was decided to retain a more conventional straight wing arrangement, although de Havilland would claim that the new wing on the DH.112 was swept because of its 17-degree tapering leading edge. It clearly was not, but its thickness/chord ratio was reduced from 14 to 10 per cent.

The wing, compared to the Vampire's, also had a greater area of 279 sq/ft. It was also designed to carry a 78-gallon fuel tank on each wing tip and had a pylon under each side capable of holding a 1,000lb bomb, an additional fuel tank or a pair of rocket pods. There was very little room for the undercarriage in the new wing and, after much deliberation and modification, the wheels were made thinner but had a large diameter with the tyres inflated to a much higher pressure. Even after these time-consuming changes, the undercarriage still caused bulges above and below the wing in the retracted position despite Dunlop producing a single-disc hydraulic brake. Other changes included a revised fuel system to handle up to four external fuel tanks, spring-tab controls and bigger boundary-layer deflectors in front of the air intakes.

Two aircraft, VV612 and VV613, were extracted from the Vampire FB.5 production line and transported to Hatfield to become the DH.112 prototypes in mid-1949. It was at this stage that the name Venom was finally adopted, only weeks before the first aircraft, VV612, made its maiden flight from Hatfield on 2 September 1949, just in time for that year's SBAC at Farnborough. The final aircraft only differed slightly from the original DH.112 design by having an extended tailplane, outboard of the fins while the flaps and airbrakes were also slightly modified. All in all, the Venom was a huge improvement over the Vampire and quickly established itself as being a better aircraft and quicker than the Meteor F.8. VV613 first flew on 23 July 1950 and the only change it introduced was wing fences to prevent tip stall and high angles of attack. This problem was rectified further by adding a horizontal fin to the wing tip tanks and small slats on the inner leading edge of the tank, complete with strake, which flowed up from the wing.

The Venom's performance excelled in all departments, with manoeuvrability, rate of climb, ceiling and stability as a gun platform, being praised by all.

Massed-produced fighter

In early 1950, full production of the Venom was authorised and exciting plans were made for the Venom, along with the Republic F-84, to become the standard NATO fighter-bombers. A scheme was drawn up at the Palais de Chaillot for more than 2,000 Venoms to be built, with 1,185 being produced in the UK by de Havilland, Bristol and Fairey. On the continent, assembly centres were to be established by Macchi and Fiat in Italy as the Fiat G.81, and Sud-Aviation in France, which was already building the Vampire as the SE.535 Mistral. Unfortunately, this ambitious idea, which would have seen the Venom become as common a sight in European skies as the F-84 never came to fruition, thanks to the debilitating decline in the British aviation industry at the time.

The first of 17 RAF squadrons to receive the Venom FB.1 (replacing the Vampire FB.5) was 11 Squadron at Wünstorf in August 1952. (*Aeroplane*)

Into RAF service

Orders for the RAF were drastically cut back, but eventually 375 Venom FB.1s (serialled WE255–483, WK389–503 and WR272–373) entered service; the first with 11 Squadron at Wünstorf, West Germany, in August 1952, as part of the 2nd TAF. The new jet was initially received with enthusiasm by RAF pilots but after a few aircraft were lost to structural failure, some doubts began to creep in. A stringent +2G manoeuvre limitation was imposed and the lack of an ejection seat and air conditioning saw the Venom's honeymoon period come to an abrupt end. The aircraft's poor roll rate was also criticised but, on the whole, the Venom was an equal to the straight-wing F-84 at all heights and was on a par with the Ouragan. However, when it came to taking on a Canberra, the Venom was outclassed, and an F-86 was in a different league.

The Venom FB.1 served with several squadrons in West Germany, the Middle East and Far East and after the initial limitations were removed, was accepted with muted praise by many service pilots. But the lack of ejection seats, accompanied by a steady flow of accidents, many resulting from further structural failures, forced de Havilland to consider developing the Venom still further. Thus, the FB.4 was born when a modified FB.1, WE381 was first flown 29 December 1953.

The prototype Venom NF.2, WP227 (ex G-5-3), which made its maiden flight on 22 August 1950. Ordered as a one-off for evaluation, the Venom only served with the A&AEE and in September 1953 became an instructional airframe at RAF Locking. (Via Martyn Chorlton)

The FB.4 was an attempt to rectify all of the original mark's serious deficiencies starting with the fitment of a Martin Baker Mk I ejection seat and a Godfrey air-conditioning system. A descent rate of roll was introduced by installing a set of hydraulically boosted ailerons and the rudders were now also powered. The tail was aerodynamically improved with front and rear-facing bullets and the fins and rudders were also enlarged. The FB.4 was a considerably more purposeful aircraft, but it was now the mid-1950s and the Venom had sadly missed its chance, as slippery jets such as the Hunter were leading the field.

The first of 150 FB.4s (serialled WR374–564) entered service in 1955 and, along with the Hunter, quickly replaced the FB.1 in Europe, the Middle and Far East. The FB.4 went on to see a great deal of action in Aden, Cyprus, Malaya, Oman and Suez and proved to be useful ground-attack aircraft thanks to its decent payload and four 20mm guns in the nose. 28 Squadron was the last Venom unit, retiring the type in favour of the Hunter FGA.9 in July 1962.

Venom night-fighter

The night-fighter version of the Venom began as a private venture, with hopes, like the Vampire NF.10, being pinned on overseas orders rather than from the RAF. Following the pattern of the evolution of the Vampire NF.10, the prototype Venom night-fighter made use of the wings and tail-booms from the FB.1, mounted onto a new wider and longer fuselage pod. Designated as the Venom NF.2, the prototype WP227 (ex G-5-3) made its maiden flight on 22 August 1950. Just like the Vampire NF.10, the fuselage featured a longer nose to accommodate an AI-type radar although the fuselage was made slightly wider so that the crew positions were not staggered. Despite the wider fuselage, neither the NF.2, or its succeeding mark would ever be fitted with ejection seats, much to the disappointment of the RAF.

However, the Venom NF.2 was deemed as a better aircraft than the in-service Meteor NF.11 and Vampire NF.10, and an order for 90 aircraft was placed by the RAF. This included a pre-production batch of seven aircraft, serialled WL804–810, which were delivered from Hatfield in September and October 1952. The remainder, built in two batches (WL811–874 and WR779–808) at Chester and to a lesser extent at Hatfield were delivered between November 1952 and April 1955.

The Venom NF.2 first entered RAF service in November 1953 with 23 Squadron at Coltishall, replacing the Vampire NF.10s. While the Venom was an improvement over its predecessor, all was not well with the aircraft, which suffered from a wide range of technical snags that resulted in flying restrictions being imposed on the night fighter. The problems were slowly ironed out, but so many modifications were needed, a sub-variant, the NF.2A was introduced. This variant featured the same frameless canopy fitted to the Vampire T.11 and raked fins.

23 Squadron was destined to be the only unit to operate the original Venom NF.2, while three more squadrons were reformed with the NF.2A. These were 33 and 219 squadrons stationed at Driffield and 253 Squadron at Waterbeach between April and October 1955.

A third and final variant of the Venom, the NF.3, sought to rectify all of the problems encountered by the NF.2 and NF.2A during operational service. The main improvement over the earlier marks was an AI.21 radar, which was basically a Westinghouse AN/APS-57 supplied to Britain as part of the US Military Assistance Program. The NF.3 also introduced a hinged radome, rather than a sliding type, powered ailerons, redesigned rudders and a frameless canopy with a powered jettison system.

An order for 129 Venom NF.3s was placed, all being built at Christchurch with deliveries beginning in September 1953. However, the NF.3 (serialled WX785–949 and WZ315–320) did not enter service until June 1955 with 141 Squadron at Coltishall, followed by, 23, 151, 125 and 89 squadrons in January 1956. The NF.2A remained in service until September 1957 when 253 Squadron was disbanded, and like the Vampire NF.10 before it, the service life of the Venom night fighters was short. All of the Vampire NF.3s were withdrawn in 1957, the last of them by 89 Squadron in November at Stradishall, making way for the next generation of jet, the Gloster Javelin.

De Havilland Thin-Wing Vampire

De Havilland's brochure for its Thin Wing Vampire proposal was dated 31 March 1948. The initial drawing showed the aircraft powered by a de Havilland Ghost engine, which would require air intakes 10 per cent larger than those used by the original Vampire. This project eventually became the Venom and the brochure's Introduction stated:

> With the present emphasis on high-altitude interception, an investigation has been made into the possibility of a further development of the Vampire by fitting a Ghost engine and a thin wing. The present RAF fighters will be in service for the next five to six years and it will take time to get a new fighter, currently at the preliminary stage, into service use, therefore, everything possible should be done to develop the current jet fighters as high-altitude interceptors.
>
> The Vampire is particularly suitable for high-altitude work because of its low-wing loading, good manoeuvrability and small turning circle. The thin wing improves the Mach performance and makes use of the extra power of the Ghost at high altitude. A Vampire has been flying with a Ghost engine installed for ten months and there is nothing experimental about the proposed

The second prototype Venom, VV613, which was first flown on 23 July 1950. The second prototype introduced wing fences to stop wing tip stall and horizontal fins to the wing-tip fuel tanks. (*Aeroplane*)

changes – the engine itself is a scaled-up Goblin and we would need to modify the existing Ghost Vampire prototype with a thin wing.

It was predicted that fitting the Ghost in a thin-wing Vampire would increase the weight by about 600lb. The estimated data for the new aircraft* with a Ghost giving 5,000lb of thrust, included a take-off weight of 10,924lb, a sea-level rate of climb of 8,050ft/min, operational ceiling 50,500ft, sea level to 40,000ft would take 10.3 minutes, and the maximum speed at sea level would be 609mph and at 45,000ft 524mph. A 5,500lb-thrust version of the new engine would increase these figures to 10,972lb, 9,650ft/min, 52,000ft, 8.8 minutes, 615mph and 529mph.

On April 14, Air Commodore John Boothman at the Air Ministry wrote 'on the face of it, this is a very attractive proposition in that it will improve the Vampire for the last few years of its life'. On July 15, WA Coryton added;

With regard to whether de Havilland could undertake the work without detriment in terms of time to its existing

DH.112 Venom FB.1

Engine	4,850lb de Havilland Ghost 103
Span	41ft 8in
Length	31ft 10in
Height	6ft 2in
Wing area	279 sq/ft
Loaded weight	15,400lb
Max speed	597 mph
Initial climb	7,230ft/min
Service ceiling	48,000ft
Range	1,075 miles with tip tanks
Armament	Four x 20mm Hispano V and eight x 60lb RP.3 or two 1,000lb

DH.112 Venom NF.3

Engine	4,950lb de Havilland Ghost 104
Span	42ft 10in
Length	36ft 8in
Height	7ft 2in
Wing area	279sq/ft
Empty weight	11,300lb
Loaded weight	15,480lb
Max speed	595mph
Initial climb	6,450ft/min
Service ceiling	45,000ft
Range	1,000 miles
Armament	Four x 20mm Hispano V

Vampire: De Havilland's First Generation Twin-Boom Jet Fighter

The sole export version of the Venom night fighter was the NF.51 (based on the NF.2) of which 60 were sold to Sweden, which operated the type from 1953 to 1960 as the J33. (Via Martyn Chorlton)

RAF commitments, it would seem that the rib and spar design and method of attaching the covering will be exactly similar to the Vampire, no new fundamental design principles are introduced, and there is no need to direct high-grade design staff. De Havilland may go ahead even without our support as the aircraft will find a ready sale as an interceptor in foreign markets.

The new type did indeed go ahead and was named Venom during the summer of 1949.

MINISTRY DIARY FOR VENOM FB.1/FB.4, 1948–55

1948

April	De Havilland submitted a brochure containing proposals for a development of the Vampire with a thinner wing and a 5,000lb static-thrust Ghost engine instead of the standard Goblin.
September	The Air Staff approved the thin-wing Vampire and this became known as the Vampire FB.8, and later the Venom FB.1. Apart from the new wing and engine installation, this aircraft also required a new undercarriage and a strengthened tail.
November	De Havilland was instructed to proceed with the supply of two prototype aircraft plus some strength test specimens.

1949

July	A production order was placed for 200 FB.1 Venoms.
September	The first prototype made its maiden flight.

1950

February	The production order was reduced by 116 FB.1 (leaving a total of 84) to await the 'type approval' for the Ghost engine (the reduction was restored in October 1950).
March	Structural tests commenced on the aircraft's wing.
May	The first prototype went to A&AEE Boscombe Down to undergo preview handling trials.

July	The second prototype made its maiden flight; this aircraft was subsequently used for engine flight testing and for de Havilland's own development flying.
August	Due to delays caused by aircraft and engine un-serviceability, it was decided to advance the first two production machines as much as possible.
September	The first prototype returned from Boscombe to de Havilland and began resonance tests with wing tip tanks. This aircraft was later used for engine flight development.
November	The first production aeroplane flew and was allotted to de Havilland to clear the carriage of external stores. In the meantime, the second prototype continued its development flying on handling characteristics, which included the effect of having wing-tip tanks.
December	The production contract was increased by 205 FB.1s, making the total now on order 405.

1951

March	The second production aircraft first flew and was allotted for cabin conditioning and other engineering work. The second prototype was now engaged on wing-tip tank problems. The production order was increased again by 400 (805 FB.1s).
July	The first production aircraft went to A&AEE for handling trials with external stores and also for gunnery trials. In fact, the latter was given priority since the type's clearance as an interceptor was required first. The production order increased again by 341 (total now 1,146 FB.1).
August	The type's handling characteristics at high-Mach numbers was criticised by A&AEE so investigations commenced initially to provide warnings, and later for improved characteristics. Production order now reduced by 34 (1,112).
October	Owing to some canopy failures experienced on de Havilland Vampires in RAF service, the provision of satisfactory canopies for both the Vampire and Venom was put in hand with some urgency. A trail installation of power-operated ailerons to improve the aircraft's rolling performance was also started.

1952

February	Three aircraft were cleared for trials with the Central Fighter Establishment (CFE).
March	Two aircraft were prepared for rocket interceptor simulation trials at CFE. The production order was reduced again by 162 (total now 950 FB.1).
May	A pre-release clearance was issued for a limited number of Venoms to permit crew familiarisation and intensive flying trials to begin, but these aircraft were not allowed to carry rockets or bombs.
September	Controller Aircraft (CA) Release was issued to allow the carriage of rockets, but not bombs.

1953

April	Following a brief Boscombe Down trial on a trial installation aircraft, it was decided that power-operated ailerons should be introduced on the Venom as soon as possible. In due course, Venoms with power-operated ailerons were later designated FB.4s.
August	Several FB.1s were found to have cracks in the wing skin in front of the cut-out for the undercarriage, and consequently a modification to strengthen the wing at this point

	was introduced. Once again, the production order was cut, this time by 300 leaving a total of 650.
December	Some complaints were made by the RAF that the elevator-control forces had shown an increase on later aircraft. An investigation was opened and in due course a modification was introduced.

1954

March	Severe cracking of the wing skin was discovered behind the undercarriage cut-out, and ground attack operations were therefore banned until some strengthening modifications had been incorporated. The FB.1 production order was reduced by a further 127 (total now 523).
April	Due to a series of fires being experienced in the air, the manufacturer started an investigation of the air flow on the under fuselage. CA Release was now extended to include the carriage of some types of bomb.
May	The first production FB.4 was sent to A&AEE for handling trials. The production contract was amended to 372 FB.1 and 151 FB.4 (in November the Mk.1 figure was reduced by 1 to 371).
July	The FB.4 trials, having been delayed by aircraft un-serviceability, were now halted entirely pending the cure of aileron flutter, which had been experienced on the NF.3 night-fighter version of the Venom.
August	The FB.4 trials were restarted, but aircraft now had to be returned to the manufacturer because the elevator control forces were found to be unacceptable.
October	To meet some A&AEE criticism, action was taken on the FB.4 to modify the hydraulic system used for the power-controlled ailerons to provide earlier warning of power failures.
November	Because of further fires in the air, flying was severely restricted until 16 essential modifications had been introduced for all Venom marks.

1955

January	A&AEE's handling trials on the FB.4 were concluded.

Chapter 13
Venom

All Venoms built for the RAF, and Sea Venoms for the Fleet Air Arm between 1949 and January 1958 are listed below.

Venom
De Havilland Aircraft Co, Hatfield, Herts

Venom prototypes — VV612 and VV613 (2) converted from FB.5; VV612, f/f 2 Sep 1949
Venom FB.1 (200) — WE255–294, WE303–389, WE399–438 and WE444–483, delivered between Jun 1951 and Dec 1953 to Contract 6/Acft/3627
Venom FB.1 (85) — WK389–437 and WK468–503, delivered between Mar 1954 and Mar 1955 to Contract 6/Acft/6062
Venom FB.1 (90) — WR272–321 and WR334–373, delivered between Apr 1955 and Mar 1956 to Contract 6/Acft/6400
Venom NF.2 (7) — WL804–810, delivered in Sep and Oct 1952 to Contract 6/Acft/6137
Venom NF.2 (1) — WP227 (Ex G-5-3), delivered to A&AEE to Contract 6/Acft/6323
Venom NF.3 (1) — WV928, delivered to RAF in Mar 1955 as instructional airframe No.7189M
Venom NF.4 (150) — WR374–509 and WR525–56, four delivered between Mar 1955 and Mar 1956 to Contract 6/Acft/6400

De Havilland Aircraft Co, Hawarden/Broughton, Chester
Venom NF.2 (53) — WL811–833 and WL845–87, four delivered between Nov 1952 and Apr 1955 to Contract 6/Acft/6137

De Havilland Aircraft Co, Hatfield and Chester
Venom NF.2 (30) — WR779–808, delivered between Jul 1954 and Jan 1955 to Contract 6/Acft/6401. WR809–820, WR835–880 and WR897–908 were cancelled

De Havilland Aircraft Co, Christchurch, Hants
Venom NF.3 (123) — WX785–810, WX837–886 and WX903–949, delivered between Sep 1953 and Mar 1956 to Contract 6/Acft/7162
Venom NF.3 (6) — WZ315–320, delivered between Mar and May 1956 to Contract 6/Acft/7339. WZ321–WZ348 were cancelled

Sea Venom

De Havilland Aircraft Co, Hatfield
Sea Venom NF.20 — (2) Prototypes WK376 and WK379, built in Experimental Department and delivered May 1951 and Sep 1952 respectively to Contract 6/Acft/5972/CB.7a

De Havilland Aircraft Co, Christchurch, Hants

Sea Venom NF.20 (1)	Third prototype WK385 laid down at Hatfield and completed at Christchurch to Contract 6/Acft/5972/CB.7(a)
Sea Venom FAW.20 (12)	WM500–504, WM507–511, WM515 and WM518, delivered between Mar 1953 and Mar 1954 to Contract 6/Acft/3974/CB.7(b)
Sea Venom FAW.21 (8)	WM568 and WM570–576, delivered between Apr 1954 and Mar 1955 to Contract 6/Acft/6165/CB.7(a)
Sea Venom FAW.21 (32)	WW138, WW140, WW143–147, WW149, WW151, WW153, WW186, WW188, WW190, WW193, WW195–199, WW209–211, WW219–220, WW261–263, WW274 and WW295–298
Sea Venom FAW.53 (49)	WZ893–911 and WZ927–946 for Royal Australian Navy, delivered on HMAS *Melbourne* 11 Mar 1956, arriving Sydney 9 May 1956.
Sea Venom FAW.21 (1)	Prototype XA539, delivered to A&AEE 3 Jun 1954 to Contract 6/Acft/7062/CB.7(a)
Sea Venom FAW.21(26)	XG606–624, XG663, XG666–667, XG669, XG672, XG674, XG677 and XG679, delivered between Jan and Jul 1956 to Contract 6/Acft/10501/CB.7(a)
Sea Venom FAW.22 (1)	XG685, delivered 4 Dec 1956 to Contract 6/Acft/10501/CB.7(a)

Eleven RAF squadrons operated the Venom FB.4 including 6 Squadron, which received the type in place of the FB.1 at Habbaniyah, Iraq, in June 1955. Delivered in 1955, WR413 was later transferred to 208 Squadron until March 1960 when the aircraft was SOC. (Via Martyn Chorlton)

De Havilland Aircraft Co, Hawarden/Broughton, Chester

Sea Venom FAW.20 (38) WM505–506, WM512–514, WM516–517, WM519–523 and WM542–567, delivered between May 1954 and Jun 1955 to Contract 6/Acft/3974/CB.7(b)

Sea Venom FAW.21 (2) WM569 and WM577, delivered in Apr 1954 and Apr 1955 to Contract 6/Acft/6165/CB.7(a)

Sea Venom FAW.21 (64) WW137, WW139, WW141–142, WW148, WW150, WW152, WW154, WW187, WW189, WW191–192, WW194, WW200–208, WW212–218, WW221–225, WW264–273 and WW275–294, delivered between Apr 1955 and Feb 1956 to Contract 6/Acft/6165/CB.7(a)

Sea Venom FAW.21 (34) XG625–638, XG653–662, XG664–665, XG668, XG670–673, XG675–676, XG678 and XG680, delivered between Mar and Oct 1956 to Contract 6/Acft/10501/CB.7(a)

Sea Venom FAW.22 (39) XG681–702 and XG721–737, delivered between Nov 1956 and Jan 1958 to Contract 6/Acft/10501/CB.7(a)

The second prototype DH.112 Venom, VV613, which was retained by the manufacturer for a variety of trials. Originally built as an FB.5 by English Electric, the prototype of the thin-wing Vampire was designated as the Vampire 8. (*Aeroplane*)

Chapter 14
A Venom to Heaven

An 8 Squadron Venom FB.4 starts its Goblin engine at Salalah, Oman, in 1960. 8 Squadron operated the Venom from March 1955 through to January 1960.

Tony Haig-Thomas recounts his experience of flying the Venom:

Punching a hole in the night sky
It is an overcast night. The date is 15 July 1959 and I am 21; there is an all-pervasive and suffocating heat that only those who have lived in Aden can imagine. I drag down the harness in my Venom FB.4 until it bites into my shoulders and my hands run around the familiar pre-start cockpit drills. Then, moments later, the stillness is shattered by the cartridge starter, and the dark is replaced by an orange glow behind me as the Ghost engine lights up, a little wet, and for a few seconds, the flickering light of hot jet fuel illuminates the ground crew standing by the aircraft. The distinctive wailing sound of the engine, so common in the forties and fifties on airfields throughout the world, rises in pitch as I move slowly out of the 8 Squadron dispersal, down the long taxiway, to Khormaksar's main runway. Minutes later, safely airborne and off the noisy airfield frequency, the Venom punches a satisfying hole in the night sky at 360 knots; the soft glow from the instruments, under ultra-violet stimulation, absorbs my total attention as I close at 10,000ft/min on the 8/8 cloud cover.

A tropical moon
It is just a sheet of stratus at 2,000ft and I do not expect it to be thick. Even so I am quite unprepared to be through it in a few seconds to erupt on a world so breathtaking that the memory of it will remain with me all my life. A huge tropical full moon has risen and it is poised just a few inches above a sea of cloud that stretches to the horizon; my eyes, having accommodated to the darkness below, are particularly well-adapted to absorb the scene

completely. Easing back on the throttle I roll gently round the huge white orb and go low flying over the moonlit ocean until, in all too short a time, the fuel gauge shows 1,400lbs remaining from the 2,750lb that I took off with. For this sortie, my tip tanks have not been filled. I still have my briefed exercise to fly and, sadly, this does not include low flying over my private moonlit sea. I am to climb to 20,000ft, home to overhead my base at Khormaksar, just north of Aden, and then, after a controlled let down, to feed into a radar approach. A low-level overshoot is then to be flown from the runway threshold, with this followed by a turn down wind and a full-stop landing to complete the sortie.

Centrifugal engines, like the Ghost in my Venom, need very careful handling as there is no automatic acceleration control unit fitted and I need energy, which is speed, so I open the engine up slowly and smoothly to full power. The Venom now races low level across the sea towards the moon and, very soon, I have 0.65 indicated on my Mach meter so I pull smoothly back on the stick until 4G is registered on the accelerometer. The aircraft passes the vertical, the G loading falls off, and I am then facing back, down-moon, into a dark night sky. A short pause in the inverted, a deft left deflection of the stick with my right wrist, to roll upright and I am now heading in the general direction of my base. I can relax now, settle down to some instrument flying, and just do as the controller tells me, until the lights at the end of the runway appear, at which time more demanding handling skills will again be required of me.

En route to Aden in May 1959, taken at Kano, Nigeria.

'Khormaksar overhead'

Now, on the ground at Khormaksar, every time I transmit, a little line will jump out from the centre of the controller's cathode-ray tube and, where it touches the circumference of his circular display, will be a number. This is the heading, in degrees, that I have to steer to guide me to the 'Khormaksar

Ground engineers tend to Venom FB.4, WR554, of 8 Squadron at Khormaksar, seemingly oblivious to local military presence.

overhead'. I follow my instructions and within three or four minutes, the controller again asks me to transmit. I do so and the little line on his tube wavers around the central spot indicating that I am overhead my base. The controller gives me an 'outbound' heading to steer and, a minute later, tells me to commence my descent. In the dark, still, silence of my cockpit I reduce my RPM to 6,000 and extend the airbrakes; a gentle vibration of the airframe tells me that they are deployed. The airspeed bleeds to 270kts at which point I lower the nose and hold this speed until, at 12,000ft, I start a left turn to align me with Khormaksar's runway 09. Now I am heading back up-moon and sinking fast to the layer of cloud; the Goddess herself is a little higher on the horizon but the wondrous sight is still there. I take a few seconds off my instruments to drink it in once more and then, like Count Dracula returning to the grave after a brief night of joy, I descend into the cloud.

GCA radar approach

Down on the ground the approach controller presses a 'talk' switch on an intercom to the radar operator. 'I have a Venom at five miles, level at 2,000ft, steering 090 degrees.'

The approach controller waits until he has confirmation that the approach radar has me in good contact and then tells me to change my radio to the radar frequency. Operators of what was, in those days, called a GCA radar always had a wonderful, reassuring, level tone to their instructions. Tonight, the quiet reassuring voice tells me to reduce speed and carry out my checks for landing. Back in the cockpit I emerge from the base of the cloud and, in the few seconds I allow myself off my instruments, I can see the lights of Aden town dimly through the heat haze. I lower half flap, and then the undercarriage, feeling, as always, relief when I see the three little green lights appear to show that the wheels are down and locked. When the speed gets to 120kts I hold it there, with a little more power, at 8,000RPM.

The GCA Controller starts his patter. 'Venom you are at five miles on centre line and approaching the glide path – do not acknowledge any further instructions.' I again do as I am told and, at two miles, in the haze, I can just see the runway lights. 'Venom, final check, confirm three greens.'

'Three greens,' I reply.

'Roger. Continue your descent, on centre line, and on glide path.' Tonight, in the heat, the wind has fallen to a calm and this makes it easy, both for myself and the controller. At one mile

A pair of 8 Squadron Venom FB.4s kick up the dust at Salalah, a staging post in the Sultanate of Muscat and Oman in the coastal plain of Dhofar, 650 miles from Aden.

and around 300ft, with the runway lights now clearly visible, I dispense with the controller's instructions and continue visually. He keeps up his steady monologue although his voice has now become just background noise. I select full flap and cross the runway threshold 5kts fast, at 110kts, holding the aircraft steady with my right hand, while my left smoothly applies power. The engine produces 5,200lbs of thrust at full power and my aircraft, with its fuel state now down to 800lbs, only weighs around 9,000lbs so the acceleration, for an aircraft of its time, is very good; I raise my flaps to half-way and then the undercarriage. Although I am now back on instruments, through my peripheral vision, I feel, rather than see, the runway lights flashing past, and then blurring, to become a continuous stream of light.

Suddenly I have left the airfield. Ahead, if I look out, is an inky blackness for I am now over the sea. Looking out at 300ft and 190kts in an inky blackness, with nothing in front of me except the sea, is a sure way of dying, I again fly my aircraft on instruments. The radar controller hands me over to the tower as I turn through 180 degrees, and now at 1,000ft on the runway's reciprocal heading, I call 'Venom down wind'. It is a point of principle in the single-seat world to keep all RT transmissions as brief and clipped as possible so I avoid any unnecessary words. I complete my circuit visually, land, and taxi in, plunging back into the sauna heat of an Aden night as I open the hood and look for the marshaller's wands to guide me to my parking place. As I shut the high-pressure cockpit the wailing banshee behind me dies. My hands run through the familiar shut down procedure and the ground crew appear and replace the pin in my ejection seat.

'Aircraft all right sir?'

'Yes,' I reply, wondering if it was possible for life to get any better.

A five-ship Vampire FB.1 formation from 73 Squadron operating out of Habbaniyah, Iraq, in the summer of 1954. WK482 was one of several FB.1s later transferred to the RNZAF. (*Aeroplane*)

Chapter 15

All-Weather Sea Hornet Replacement

De Havilland Sea Venom FAW.21 XG612 during Ghost 104/105 engine, catapult and arrester gear trials in February 1956. The aircraft was also later used for Blue Jay/Firestreak trials before serving with 700 Squadron at Ford. (Via Owen Cooper)

A new night fighter for the FAA

In early 1948, at the beginning of the DH.112 programme, de Havilland conducted a study on carrier-based variants of the Venom. The study took a more serious turn when Admiralty specification N.107 was issued calling for a Sea Hornet NF.21 replacement. At the same time, the Venom was being considered for a career at the sea, the DH.110, later more familiarly known as the Sea Vixen, was already being developed and its swept-wing design was seen by many as the way forward, while the

The second prototype Sea Venom NF.20 in July 1952 with long-stroke main undercarriage legs, an arrestor hook (extended fuselage can just be seen above the tail-pipe), catapult hooks and the same tail section as the Venom NF.3. (Via Owen Cooper)

The third prototype Sea Venom NF.20, WK385, demonstrating the hydraulically folding wings at Christchurch in January 1953. (Via Owen Cooper)

comparatively straight wing of the Venom, was not. The Sea Vixen's day would come; the aircraft later serving alongside its straight-winged sibling for several years.

In the meantime, the prototype Venom NF.2, WP227 was being used to carry out deck-landing trials, although these were only 'touch-and-goes' as no arrestor hook was fitted to this aircraft. The trial went well enough for de Havilland to proceed with a navalised prototype NF.2, which it designated as the Sea Venom NF.20, serialled WK376; the aircraft was built in the Experimental Department at Hatfield to Contract 6/Acft/5972/CB.7a and made its maiden flight on 19 April 1951.

Into production

Production of the Sea Venom was allocated to Airspeed at Christchurch and at Chester, but not before two more prototypes were built at Hatfield. These were second prototype WK379 (also built in the Experimental Department), which featured long-stroke main undercarriage legs, an arrestor hook, catapult hooks and the same tail section as the Venom NF.3. A third prototype, WK385, which was laid down at Hatfield, but completed at Christchurch, was fitted with hydraulically folding wings and an AI Mk 10 radar in the nose.

The first production aircraft, now designated as the Sea Venom FAW.20 (the FAW standing for Fighter All-Weather), WM500, made is maiden flight from Christchurch on 27 March 1953. Out of the 50 FAW.20s built, only a dozen were constructed at Christchurch (WM500–504, WM507–511, WM515 and WM518) while the remainder (WM505–506, WM512–514, WM516–517, WM519–523 and WM542–567) were built at Chester.

Operational service

The FAW.20 entered operational service with 890 Squadron, which reformed at Yeovilton on 20 March 1954, with nine Sea Venoms on strength. After carrying out Deck Landing Practice (DLP) on HMS *Bulwark* the squadron set sail aboard HMS *Albion* from July to September 1955, but by the following month the unit was relegated to the second line and was renumbered as 766 Squadron, operating from Yeovilton. 809 and 891 squadrons also received the Sea Venom FAW.20 in 1955, followed by 808 Royal Australian Navy in 1955, and finally 700 Squadron in September 1956. The latter, reformed at Ford on 18 August 1956, was a Trials and Requirements Unit with a variety of aircraft on strength. By the time the first Sea Venoms arrived, the unit had moved to Yeovilton following the closure of Ford. The last Sea Venom FAW.20s saw out their days with 700 Squadron; the last examples being retired in 1959.

The Sea Venom FAW.20s of 890 Squadron on the line at Yeovilton in 1954. Reformed on 20 March 1954, WM516 '205'VL' (nearest the camera) was delivered to the unit in August 1954. (*Aeroplane*)

FAW.22, XG697 '732/VL' in service with Airwork ADTU at Yeovilton circa 1966. One of the longer serving examples of the Sea Venom; the aircraft retired in 1968 with 1,722 flying hours (high for a Sea Venom). (Via Owen Cooper)

Although the FAW.20 featured a better visibility canopy and improved tail, the aircraft was fitted with manual ailerons, which made the Sea Venom a sluggish performer, especially in the roll. The next variant, the Sea Venom FAW.21 would have improved handling thanks to power-boosted rudders and ailerons. The FAW.21 also featured a Westinghouse AI Mk 21 radar, Maxaret non-skid brakes and a Ghost Mk 104 engine.

In total, 167 Sea Venom FAW.21s were built at Christchurch and Chester; the former in four batches, of eight (WM568 and WM570–576), 32 (WW138, WW140, WW143–147, WW149, WW151, WW153, WW186, WW188, WW190, WW193, WW195–199, WW209–211, WW219–220, WW261–263, WW274 and WW295–298), 26 (XG606–624, XG663, XG666–667, XG669, XG672, XG674, XG677 and XG679) and one (XA539). The latter was the FAW.21 prototype, which was delivered to A&AEE on 3 June 1954 to Contract 6/Acft/7062/CB.7(a). At Chester, the FAW.21 was built in four batches of two (WM569 and WM577), 64 (WW137, WW139, WW141–142, WW148, WW150, WW152, WW154, WW187, WW189, WW191–192, WW194, WW200–208, WW212–218, WW221–225, WW264–273 and WW275–294) and 34 (XG625–638, XG653–662, XG664–665, XG668, XG670–673, XG675–676, XG678 and XG680). A further 39 Sea Venoms were built as FAW.53s (WZ893–911 and WZ927–946) for the RAN, all delivered to HMAS *Melbourne* on 11 March 1956 and arriving in Sydney on 9 May.

A realistic chance of escape

From the 100th production FAW.21 onwards, the Sea Venom was finally installed with a pair of Martin-Baker Mk 4A ejection seats. An additional safety feature was a rapid-inflation seat pack, which gave added thrust should the two crew have to evacuate under water. The canopy above the pilot's head was also fitted with a bulge to give more clearance above his 'bone dome'.

The first unit to receive the Sea Venom FAW.21 was 809 Squadron, which was reformed at Yeovilton on 7 May 1956 with nine aircraft on strength. After carrying out DLP on HMS *Bulwark* in July, the unit joined HMS *Albion* in the Mediterranean on 15 September 1956. During November, the unit took part in Suez operations (Operation *Musketeer*), which included attacks against Egyptian airfields, tanks and various military vehicles totalling 138 sorties. 809 Squadron retained the FAW.21 until it was disbanded on 17 August 1959. 1955 also saw FAW.21s delivered to 787, 891 and 892 squadrons; the latter also taking part in Suez, operating from HMS *Eagle*. Three more units received the FAW.21 in 1956; 700, 890 and 893 followed in 1957 by 894, 736 and 738 squadrons. In FAA service, the FAW.21 saw out its days with 750 Squadron, an Observer School at Hal Far, Malta. The type arrived in July 1960 but was quickly superseded by the FAW.22 and was retired by October 1961.

The FAW.53 first saw service from June 1955 with 724 (RAN) Squadron, a pilot conversion unit based at Nowra. The unit operated an average of five Sea Venom FAW.53s, which gave reliable service until they were withdrawn in 1973, in favour of the MB.326H. Operationally, the FAW.53 served with 805, 808 and 816 (RAN) squadrons from February 1956 until August 1967 making way for the A-4 Skyhawk and the S-2 Tracker.

The best of the breed

The later version of the FAW.21 had turned the Sea Venom into a good aircraft, but there was still room for a final tweak or two, which would make the FAW.22 the best of the breed. Ejection seats were fitted as standard, while power was increased thanks to a 5,150lb Ghost Mk 105 and the radar was upgraded to an AI Mk 22. Post-delivery, several FAW.22s were converted by de Havilland to carry Blue Jay (later renamed Firestreak) air-to-air missiles, making these Sea Venoms the first aircraft to serve the FAA with an Air-to-Air Missile capability.

Only 40 FAW.22s were built, 39 of them (XG681–702 and XG721–737) were built at Chester, while XG685 was built at Christchurch.

894 Squadron was the first unit to receive the Sea Venom FAW.22 after reforming at Merryfield on 14 January 1957. After embarking on HMS *Eagle* in August, the unit spent most of 1957 and 1958 serving in the Mediterranean until returning home to Yeovilton in December 1958. Further short tours on HMS *Victorious* and *Albion* and detachments to the Far East followed, until the unit was disbanded on 17 December 1960. 891 Squadron followed in December 1957; its FAW.22s seeing service aboard HMS *Bulwark*, while 893 Squadron was the last operational unit to re-equip in January 1959 at Yeovilton. After brief service aboard HMS *Victorious*, 893 Squadron was disbanded on 29 February 1960. The final unit to receive the FAW.22, and the last bastion of the Sea Venom in FAA service, was 750 Squadron at Hal Far. The first examples arrived in August 1961 and after returning to the cooler climes of Lossiemouth in June 1965, the type served on until March 1970.

Electronic Countermeasures

The last Sea Venoms worthy of mention are the Electronic Countermeasures (ECM) variants. Seven FAW.21s were converted to ECM.21 standard while several FAW.22s became ECM.22s. Stripped of their 20mm-cannon armament, the room created was filled with a variety of ECM-type equipment and the first examples joined 751 Squadron at Watton in June 1957. Originally formed as a Radio Warfare Unit, 751 Squadron was restyled as an Electronic Warfare Unit and raised to first-line operational status on 1 May 1958 to become 831 Squadron. The ECM.21 continued to serve until October 1964, while the ECM.22, which arrived in April 1960, was not retired until May 1966.

Sea Venom FAW.22

Engine	5,300lb de Havilland Ghost 105 turbojet
Span	42ft 10in
Length	36ft 7in
Height	8ft 6¼in
Wing area	279.8sq ft
Max take-off weight	15,800lb
Max speed	575mph at sea level
Ceiling	39,500ft
Rate of climb	5,750 ft/min
Armament	Four 20mm Hispano Mk V cannons; eight 60lb RP-3 rocket projectiles; two 1,000lb bombs

A de Havilland Sea Venom is manoeuvred along the flight deck of HMS *Ark Royal* by a Douglas Tugmaster, much to the bemusement and amusement of the ground crew. (*Aeroplane*)

Chapter 16

The French North Winds Doth Blow

The Vampire FB.5s of EC 3/4 (4eme EC) 'Flandre' during its tour of duty at Friedrichshafen, circa 1950. (Via Bertrand Rouillard)

Post-war re-equipment

By December 1948, the French Armée de l'Air were receiving the first of 30 ex-RAF Vampire F.1s, followed from May 1949, by 94 ex-RAF Vampire FB.5s, which first entered service with 2eme Escadre de Chasse (EC) at Dijon. By October, the FB.5 was already in service with four escadrons: EC 1/2 Cigognes, EC 2/2 Alsace. EC 3/2 Cote-D'Or and EC 4/2 Coq Gaulois. By the following year, 3eme EC at Rheims and 4eme EC at Friedrichshafen had also been re-equipped with the Vampire FB.5, which was proving to be a popular aircraft. The French liked the Vampire so much they decided to make it their own and after some negotiation between Société Nationale de Constructions Aéronautique du Sud-Est (SNCASE) and de Havilland, a licence was issued to build 67 Vampire FB.51s in France. Components would be supplied by Hatfield for these 67 aircraft, to be assembled at Marignane, although a further agreement resulted in an extended licence allowing SNCASE to manufacture a further 120 aircraft from parts made in France. While the initial batch of 67 aircraft would be powered by Goblin engines, the French machines would be fitted with Rolls-Royce Nene 102s, built under licence by Hispano-Suiza. The first Vampire FB.51 assembled in France was No.10001 and was first flown from Marignane by Jacques Lecarme on 21 December 1950.

The SE.530, 532 and 535 Mistral

A development of a standard Vampire, the French designation for the twin-boom fighter was the SE.530 Mistral (a north-western wind that blows from the Mediterranean), while de Havilland referred to the aircraft as the FB.53. The production aircraft were redesignated as the SE.532 Mistral, the first of four pre-production prototypes (SE.530s) flying on 1 April 1951. Another 243 production aircraft followed, the first 93 of them lacking an ejection seat, while the remainder were fitted with an SNCASE seat and were redesignated as the SE.535 Mistral. It is believed that the majority of SE.532s built were later upgraded to SE.535 standard complete with an ejection seat.

Power was provided by a Nene 102B in the SE.532 and a Nene 104 in the SE.535. Both were armed with four 20mm Hispano 404 cannons and were capable of carrying eight 60lb T-10 High-Velocity Aircraft Rocket (HVAR) rockets or a pair of 1,000lb bombs.

Mistral in action

The original Vampire FB.5s and later Mistrals would fly with and fight with the same units because neither aircraft demanded unique ground-support equipment or any differing flying training. It was a Vampire unit that saw action first for the Armée de l'Air when 1eme EC based at Sidi Ahmed in Tunisia carried out missions against rebels in 1951. The unit was renumbered 7eme EC in October 1951 and in May 1953 became the first unit to receive the Mistral.

Three Mistral units saw action against rebel forces in Algeria between 1955 and 1961. These were 6eme EC at Oran, 7eme EC at Sidi Ahmed and 8eme RC at Rabat Sale. The action was never far from a Mistral's home airfield because of the aircraft's short endurance; it being insufficient for anything more than localised ground-support operations. The little Mistral did pack an appreciative punch from the French ground forces' point of view; the 20mm cannon, plus a combination of bombs, napalm and rockets were usually more than enough to dissuade their opposition. The Mistral was withdrawn from Armée de l'Air service in 1961.

Experimental Mistrals

The French conducted a large number of trials using the Vampire, but only two Mistrals, numbered 02 (the second prototype SE.530) and 061 (an SE.532) were selected for a novel experiment in 1954. Fitted with experimental oleo-pneumatic skis in place of the main undercarriage, both aircraft were trialled for Short Take-Off and Landing (STOL) tests from a specially constructed ski-slope. It is not known how successful the trial was, but it lasted from September 1954 until March 1956.

The Aquilon

Part of the French post-war military expansion was to build the aircraft carriers *Clemenceau* and *Foch*, both designed to operate piston and jet aircraft. As of 1946, the French Aéronavale did not have a 'home built' shipboard fighter of its own, so the Service Technique Aéronautique issued a requirement to French aircraft manufacturers. Unsuccessful aircraft put forward were the Aerocentre NC.1080, Arsenal VG.90 and Nord 2200, which forced the Aéronavale to look across the pond at the Grumman F9F-5 Panther.

Although seriously considered, the American fighter was deemed not suitable and instead, the Ministère de la Marine made a statement in January 1951 that it would be adopting the de Havilland Sea Venom FAW.20. The prototype would not make its first flight until April, but thanks to its experience operating and building the Vampire/Mistral, the Aéronavale was confident that it had made the right decision.

Following successful flight-testing in Britain, four pre-production Sea Venom FAW.20s were supplied by de Havilland, via Airspeed at Christchurch, to SNCASE in component form. The first aircraft, redesignated as the Aquilon 20, completed its maiden flight on 20 February 1952. A fifth Sea Venom, followed by 25 aircraft, all built from sub-assemblies supplied by Airspeed completed the production run for the Aquilon 20. It was clear that Aquilon 20 could be improved from an early stage and

SNCASE produced a single prototype named the Aquilon 201. The aircraft was based upon the Venom NF.51 and was fitted with a Fiat-built Ghost 48 engine, a pair of ejection seats and clear-view rearward sliding canopy.

The production version of the Aquilon 201 was the 202, the first making its maiden flight on 24 March 1954. The 202 featured the same 201 modifications and was also fitted with a Derveaux DRAX-4A radar rangefinder, air-conditioning and anti-skid brakes. Only 20 Aquilon 202s were built before another improved version was introduced.

A Mistral of 6eme Escadre de Chasse (EC) at Oran, during operations against rebel forces in Algeria during the late 1950s. (Via Bertrand Rouillard)

Société Nationale de Constructions Aéronautique du Sud-Est (SNCASE) built 247 production Mistrals between June and February 1953, which were simply numbered from one to 247; here, No.115 is being refuelled by Armée de l'Air ground crew. (Via Author)

The next variant, the Aquilon 203, of which 40 were built, was equipped with a Westinghouse AN/APQ-65 radar; the new equipment being first trialled in the sole Aquilon 201. The Westinghouse was a large unit that could only be fitted into the aircraft if the second ejection seat was removed, making the 203 the only single-seater in the range. The Aquilon 203 was also capable of firing a pair of Nord 5103/AA.20 radio-guided air-to-air missiles (AAM), one being carried under each wing. The aircraft was later upgraded to carry a pair of Matra R.511 semi-active radar-homing AAMs or a pair of Nord AS.20 air-to-surface missiles. All Aquilons retained the standard quartet of 20mm cannon and capability to fire unguided rocket projectiles, both of which were employed in action in Algeria during 1959. 11F and 16F naval squadrons were called upon in July 1961 at Bizerte for ground-support and air-defence operations.

The final Aquilon was the 204 radar trainer, which had its armament removed and the AN/APQ-65 radar installed. Six aircraft were converted from Aquilon 20s and because of the lack of armament, sufficient room was created to install the second seat.

The majority of Aquilons had been retired by 1960, although several were retained in a training and support role until the middle of the decade. However, it was an Aquilon that made the first landing on the *Clemenceau* on 30 March 1960, although the type's carrier-borne career was over by September 1963. The Aquilon clung on for several more years, the last flight in Aéronavale service taking place on 30 June 1966.

Aquilon 20, No.20 in service with 16F Naval Squadron at Hyères. (Via Bertrand Rouillard)

ARMÉE DE LA AIR AND AÉRONAVALE SERVICE

Armée de l'Air
2eme EC FB.5 at Dijon; **3eme EC** FB.5 at Rheims; **4eme EC** at Friedrichshafen; **EC 3/5 'Comtat-Venaissin'** F.1, FB.5 and SE.535; **EC 2/6 'Nice'** SE.535; **EC 2/7 'Nice'** FB.5; **EC 1/3 'Navarre'** FB.5; **EC 4/2 'Coqs Gaulois'** FB.5; **EC 2/2 'Alsace'** and **'Lafayette'** FB.5; **EC 4/4 'Ardennes'** FB.5; **EC 2/4 'Lafayette'** FB.5; **EC 3/4 'Flandre'** FB.5; **EC 2/5 'Ile de France'** FB.5; **EC 3/2 'Cote d'Or'** FB.5; **EC 1/2 'Cigognes'** FB.5; **Esc 2/17** FB.5; **Esc 1/5 'Vendee'** FB.5 and SE.535; **EC 1/8 'Magherb'** SE.535; **EC 2/20 'Ouarsenis'** SE.535; **EC 1/20** SE.535; **EC 1/6 'Oranie'** SE.535; **EC 2/8 'Languedoc'** SE.535; **EC 2/6 'Normandie-Niemen'** SE.535; **EC 6** SE.535; **Ecole de l'Air** SE.535; **Ecole de Chasse** FB.5; **Centre d'Essais en Vol** F.1 and SE.535; and **Le Centre d'Experimentations Aeriennes Militaries** F.1 and SE.535 at Mont de Marsan.

Aéronavale
57 Esc FB.5 at Khouribga; **2S (Aquilon)** at Lann-Bihoué; **10S (Aquilon)** at Hyères; **11F Naval Sqn (Aquilon)** at Karouba Bizerte; **16F Naval Sqn (Aquilon)** at Hyères; and **Escadrille 59S (The All-Weather Fighter Training School) (Aquilon)** at Hyères.

Armée de l'Air SNCASE SE.535 Mistrals of EC6 during the mid-1950s. The Vampire and Mistral introduced the French Air Force to jet-powered aircraft for the first time; its home grown aircraft, on this occasion, where far from suitable. (Via Martyn Chorlton)

Chapter 17
Service in All Theatres

De Havilland Vampire F.1s of 54 Squadron take off en masse at RAF Acklington in October 1947 during Armament Practice Camp. The unit operated the F.1 from October 1946, having replaced the Tempest F.2, until August 1948, when it was superseded by the Vampire F.3. (*Aeroplane*)

Vampire, Sea Vampire, Venom and Sea Venom units of the Royal Air Force and the Fleet Air Arm from March 1946 to August 1967.

Royal Air Force
First-line
3 Sqn	*Tertius primus erit (The Third shall be first)*	
A/c	Vampire F.1	Apr 1948–May 1949
	Vampire FB.5	May 1949–May 1953
Codes	J5	1946–Apr 1951
	'A'	Apr 1951–May 1953
Bases	Wünstorf, Gütersloh, Lübeck and Wildenrath	
4 Sqnn	*In futurum videre (To see into the future)*	
A/c	Vampire FB.5	Jul 1950–May 1954
	Vampire FB.9	Nov 1953–May 1954
Code	'B'	Mar 1952–1954
Bases	Wünstorf and Jever	
5 Sqn	*Frangas non flectas (Thou mayst break but shall not bend me)*	
A/c	Vampire F.3	Dec 1950–Aug 1951
	Vampire FB.5	Mar 1952–Jun 1953

Having survived the rigours of serving with 6 Squadron in the Middle East, Vampire FB.5, VV659 'D' was later transferred to 202 AFS at Valley, which was renumbered as 7 FTS on 1 June 1954. The Vampire was abandoned in a spin 2½ miles west of Valley on 16 November 1954. (*Aeroplane*)

	Venom FB.1	Nov 1952–Aug 1955
	Venom FB.4	Jul 1955–Oct 1957
Code	'B'	Mar 1952–1955
Bases	Chivenor, Llandow, Wünstorf and Fassberg	

6 Sqn *Oculi exercitus (The eyes of the Army)*
A/c	Vampire FB.5	Oct 1949–Apr 1952
	Vampire FB.9	Feb 1952–May 1954
	Venom FB.1	Feb 1954–Aug 1955
	Venom FB.4	Jun 1955–Jun 1957

Bases Deversoir, Habbaniyah, Mafraq, Nicosia, Shaibah, Abu Sueir, Sharjah, Shallufa, Amman and Akrotiri

8 Sqn *Uspiam et passim (Everywhere unbounded)*
A/c	Vampire FB.9	Dec 1952–Jul 1955
	Venom FB.1	Mar 1955–Nov 1955, Dec 1956–Apr 1957
	Venom FB.4	Oct 1955–Jan 1960

Bases Khormaksar, Sheikh Othman, Nicosia, Deversoir, Habbaniyah, Eastleigh, Khartoum and Akrotiri

11 Sqn *Ociores acrierosque aquilis (Swifter and keener than eagles)*
A/c	Vampire FB.5	Aug 1950–Dec 1952
	Venom FB.1	Aug 1952–Aug 1955
	Venom FB.4	Aug 1955–Nov 1957
Code	'L'	Apr 1951–Aug 1955
Base	Wünstorf and Fassberg	

14 Sqn	*I spread my wings and keep my promise*	
A/c	Vampire FB.5	Feb 1951–Jul 1954
	Venom FB.1	May 1953–Jun 1955
Code	'B'	May 1953–Jun 1955
Bases	Fassberg and Oldenburg	

16 Sqn	*Operta Aperta (Hidden things are revealed)*	
A/c	Vampire FB.5	Dec 1948–Jun 1954
	Venom FB.1	Jan 1954–Jun 1957
Code	EG	Apr 1946–1954
Bases	Gütersloh and Celle	

20 Sqn	*Facta non verba (Deeds not words)*	
A/c	Vampire F.1	Feb 1949–Mar 1951
	Vampire F.3	Nov 1949–Sep 1951
	Vampire FB.5	Nov 1952–Jan 1954
	Vampire FB.9	Jun 1952–Dec 1953
Code	TH	1949–1951
Bases	Llanbedr and Valley	

23 Sqn	*Semper Aggressus (Always having attacked)*	
A/c	Vampire NF.10	Sep 1951–Jan 1954
	Venom NF.2	Nov 1953–Mar 1956
	Venom NF.3	Sep 1955–May 1957
Bases	Coltishall and Horsham St Faith	

25 Sqn	*Feriens Tego (Striking I defend)*	
A/c	Vampire NF.10	Jul 1951–Feb 1954
Base	West Malling	

26 Sqn	*N wagter in die Lug (A guard in the sky)*	
A/c	Vampire FB.5	Apr 1949–Dec 1953
	Vampire FB.9	Jun 1952–Dec 1953
Codes	XC	1944–Apr 1951
	'J'	Apr 1951–Nov 1953
Bases	Gütersloh, Wünstorf and Oldenburg	

28 Sqn	*Quicquid agas age (Whatsoever you may do, do)*	
A/c	Vampire FB.5	Jan 1951–Feb 1952
	Vampire FB.9	Feb 1952–Aug 1956
	Venom FB.1	Feb 1956–Nov 1959
	Venom FB.4	Nov 1959–Jul 1962
Bases	Kai Tak and Sek Kong	

32 Sqn	*Adeste Comites (Rally round, comrades)*	
A/c	Vampire F.3	Jul 1948–Jul 1950

26 Squadron's aircraft out on the line at Wunstorf in Lower Saxony circa 1950. The squadron operated the FB.5 (seen here) and FB.9 between April 1949 and December 1953; both marks were replaced by the Sabre F.4 from November 1953. (Via Martyn Chorlton)

	Vampire FB.5	Jun 1950–Sep 1954
	Vampire FB.9	Apr 1952–Sep 1954
	Venom FB.1	Sep 1954–Jan 1957
Code	GZ	Jul 1944–May 1949
Bases	Nicosia, Shallufa, Deversoir, Kabrit, Shaibah, Ta Kali, Amman and Mafraq	

45 Sqn	*Per ardua surgo (Through difficulties I arise)*	
A/c	Vampire FB.9	May 1955–Jan 1956
	Venom FB.1	Oct 1955–Nov 1957
Code	OB	Sep 1939–May 1955
Base	Butterworth	

54 Sqn	*Audax Omnia Perpett (Boldness to endure anything)*	
A/c	Vampire F.1	Oct 1946–Aug 1948
	Vampire F.3	Apr 1948–Nov 1949
	Vampire FB.5	Oct 1949–Apr 1952
Code	HF	Nov 1945–Apr 1948
Bases	Odiham and Acklington	

60 Sqn	*Per ardua ad arthera tendo (I strive through difficulties to the sky)*	
A/c	Vampire FB.5	Dec 1950–Mar 1952
	Vampire FB.9	Mar 1952–Aug 1955
	Venom FB.1	Apr 1955–Apr 1957
	Venom FB.4	Apr 1957–Nov 1959
Base	Tengah	

67 Sqn	*No odds too great*	
A/c	Vampire FB.5	Sep 1950–Jun 1953
Code	'B'	
Bases	Gütersloh and Wildenrath	

71 (Eagle) Sqn *First from the eyries*
A/c   Vampire FB.5   Sep 1950–Oct 1953
Code   'L'
Bases   Gütersloh and Wildenrath

72 (Basutoland) Sqn *Swift*
A/c   Vampire F.1   Feb 1947–Oct 1948
         Vampire F.3   Jun 1948–Nov 1949
         Vampire FB.5   Nov 1949–May 1953
Code   FG   Jan 1947–Apr 1951
Bases   Odiham, Acklington and North Weald

73 Sqn *Tutor et Ultor (Protector and Avenger)*
A/c   Vampire F.3   Jul 1948–Oct 1950
         Vampire FB.5   May 1950–Feb 1952
         Vampire FB.9   Nov 1951–Sep 1954
         Venom FB.1   Jul 1954–Dec 1956
         Venom FB.4   Dec 1956–Mar 1957
Bases   Ta Kali, Nicosia, Castel Benito, Shaibah, Kabrit, Idris, El Adem, Habbaniyah, Deversoir, Sharjah, Muharraq, Amman, Khormaksar and Akrotiri

93 Sqn *Ad arma parati (Ready for battle)*
A/c   Vampire FB.5   Nov 1950–Apr 1954
Code   'T'
Bases   Celle and Jever

Vampire FB.5s receive some attention from their 72 Squadron ground crew at North Weald, while parked in a World War Two revetment, which still stands to this day. (*Aeroplane*)

98 Squadron quartet of Venom FB.1s out of Fassberg, West Germany, circa 1954. The unit only operated the Venom for 20 months before the arrival of the Hunter F.4 and disbandment at Jever in July 1957. (Via Martyn Chorlton)

94 Sqn   *Avenge*
A/c   Vampire FB.5   Dec 1950–Jun 1954
     Venom FB.1 Jan 1954–Sep 1957
Code   'A', Dec 1950–1955
Base   Celle

98 Sqn   *Never failing*
A/c   Vampire FB.5   Feb 1951–Aug 1953
     Venom FB.1   Aug 1953–Apr 1955
Code   'L'   Feb 1951–Apr 1955
Bases   Fassberg and Jever

112 Sqn   *Swift in destruction*
A/c   Vampire FB.5   May 1951–Feb 1954
Codes   'T', May 1951–Jul 1953
     'A', Jul 1953–Jan 1954
Bases   Fassberg, Jever and Brüggen

118 Sqn   *Occido redeoque (I kill and return)*
A/c   Vampire FB.5   May 1951–Jun 1954
     Venom FB.1   Sep 1953–May 1955
Code   'A', Apr 1951–Mar 1955
Bases   Fassberg and Jever

The famous wartime unit, 112 Squadron, was reformed at Fassberg in the fighter-bomber role with Vampire FB.5s on 12 May 1951. WA331 only served with 112 Squadron, which relinquished the FB.5 in February 1954, although this aircraft was not SOC until November 1957. (Via Martyn Chorlton)

125 (Newfoundland) Sqn
Nunquam domandi (Never to be tamed)
A/c   Venom NF.3   Dec 55–May 57
Base   Stradishall

130 (Punjab) Sqn   *Strong to Serve*
A/c   Vampire F.1   Oct 1946–Jan 1947
Code   AP   Apr 1944–1947
Base   Odiham

141 Sqn   *Caedimus Noctu (We slay by night)*
A/c   Venom NF.3   Jun 1955–Mar 1957
Base   Horsham St Faith

142 Sqn   *Determination*
A/c   Venom FB.4   Feb–Apr 1959
Base   Eastleigh

145 Sqn   *Diu Noctuque Pugnamus (We fight by day and night)*
A/c   Vampire FB.5   Mar 1952–Aug 1954
           Venom FB.1   Mar 1954–Oct 1957
Code   'B'   Mar 1952–Apr 1954
Base   Celle

141 Squadron was established as one of the RAF's premier night-fighter squadrons during World War Two and this continued when the unit was reformed at Wittering in June 1946 with the Mosquito NF.36. The Venom NF.3 joined the squadron in June 1955 and after briefly serving alongside the Meteor NF.11, was replaced by the Javelin FAW.4 in February 1957. (Via Martyn Chorlton)

151 Sqn *Foy Pour Devoir (Fidelity unto duty)*
A/c Vampire NF.10   Feb 1952–May 1953
     Venom NF.3   Sep 1955–Jun 1957
Base Leuchars

185 Sqn *Ara fejn hu (Look where it is)*
A/c Vampire FB.5   Sep 1951–May 1953
Base Hal Far, Luqa, Idris, Nicosia and Habbaniyah

208 Sqn *Vigilant*
A/c Venom FB.4   Apr 1959–Mar 1960
Base Eastleigh

213 (Ceylon) Sqn   *Irritatus Lacessit Crabro*
           (The hornet attacks when roused)
A/c   Vampire FB.5   Dec 1949–May 1952
      Vampire FB.9   Apr 1952–Sep 1954
Code AK   Apr 1939–Jan 1950
Bases Deversoir and Shallufa

As well as being the first RAF squadron to receive the Vampire F.1, 247 Squadron was also the first to receive the F.3 in July 1948. VF344 was one of the first and also went on to serve with 604, 614 and 608 squadrons until the mid-1950s. (Via Martyn Chorlton)

219 (Mysore) Sqn   *From Dusk Till Dawn*
A/c   Venom NF.2A   Sep 1955–Jul 1957
Base   Driffield

234 (Madras Presidency) Sqn   *Ignem Mortemque Despuimu*
           (We spit fire and death)
A/c   Vampire FB.5   Aug 1952–Jan 1954
           Vampire FB.9   Aug 1952–Jan 1954
Codes   'A' and 'W'   Aug 1952–Jan 1954
Base   Oldenburg

247 (China-British) Sqn   *Rise from the East*
A/c   Vampire F.1   Mar 1946–May 1949
           Vampire F.3   Jul 1948–Dec 1949
           Vampire FB.5   Nov 1949–May 1952
Code   ZY   1942–Dec 1949
Base   Chilbolton, Fairwood Common, West Malling, Odiham and Acklington

249 (Gold Coast) Sqn
           Pugnis et Calcibus (With fists and heels)
A/c   Vampire FB.5   Jan 1950–May 1952
           Vampire FB.9   May 1952–Nov 1954
           Venom FB.1   Oct 1954–Nov 1955

	Venom FB.4	Jul 1955–Oct 1957
Code	GN	Oct 1945–Mar 1950
Bases	Deversoir, Nicosia, Negombo, Mafraq, Shaibah, Amman, Akrotiri, El Adem, Ta Kali, Eastleigh and Sharjah	

253 (Hyderabad State) Sqn — *Come One, Come All*
A/c	Venom NF.2A	Apr 1955–Aug 1957
Base	Waterbeach	

266 (Rhodesia) Sqn — *Hlabezulu (The stabber of the sky)*
A/c	Vampire FB.5	Aug 1952–May 1953
	Venom FB.1	Apr 1953–Aug 1955
	Venom FB.4	Jul 1955–Nov 1957
Codes	'A' and 'L'	Jul 1952–1953
Bases	Wünstorf and Fassberg	

501 (County of Gloucester) Sqn — *Nil Time (Fear nothing)*
A/c	Vampire F.1	Nov 1948–Jun 1951
	Vampire FB.5	Apr 1951–Mar 1957
	Vampire FB.9	Feb 1955–Feb 1957
Code	RAB	May 1946–1949
	SD	1949–1951
Base	Filton	

Vampire FB.5, WA303 'D' of 501 (County of Gloucester) Squadron, seen here post-1952, is given away by the boar's head emblazoned on the front of the fuselage. The unit's symbol was taken from the Gloucester coat of arms.

502 (Ulster) Sqn

		Nihil timeo (I fear nothing)
A/c	Vampire F.3	Jan 1951–Mar 1951
	Vampire FB.5	Feb 1951–Mar 1957
	Vampire FB.9	Jul 1954–Mar 1957
Code	RAC	May 1946–1949
	V9	1949–1953
Base	Aldergrove	

595 Sqn

A/c	Vampire F.1	Dec 1946–19 Oct 48
Code	7B	
Base	Pembrey	

601 (County of London) Sqn

A/c	Vampire F.3	Nov 1949–Sep 1952
Code	HT	1949–Apr 1951
Base	North Weald	

602 (City of Glasgow) Sqn

Cave Leonem Cruciatum (Beware the tormented Lion)

A/c	Vampire FB.5	Jan 1951–Mar 1957
Code	LO	1949–1953
Bases	Abbotsinch, Leuchars and Renfrew	

603 (City of Edinburgh) Sqn

	Gin ye daur (If you dare)	
A/c	Vampire FB.5	May 1951–Feb 1957
Bases	Turnhouse and Leuchars	

604 (County of Middlesex) Sqn

	Si vis pacem para bellum (If you want peace, prepare for war)	
A/c	Vampire F.3	Nov 1949–Aug 1952
Code	NG	1949–Apr 1951
Bases	North Weald	

605 (County of Warwick) Sqn

	Nunquam Dormio (I never sleep)	
A/c	Vampire F.1	Jul 1948–May 1951
	Vampire F.3	Feb 1950–Oct 1952
	Vampire FB.5	Apr 1951–Mar 1957
Code	RAL	May 1946–1949
	NR	1949–1951
Base	Honiley	

607 (County of Durham) Sqn

A/c	Vampire FB.5	Mar 1951–Mar 1957

Code	RAL	May 1946–1949
	LA	1949–Apr 1951
Base	Ouston	

608 (North Riding) Sqn
Omnibus ungulis (With all talons)

A/c	Vampire F.1	Apr 1951–Jun 1951
	Vampire F.3	May 1950–Jul 1952
	Vampire FB.5	Apr 1952–Mar 1957
	Vampire FB.9	Apr 1956–Feb 1957
Code	6T	1949–Apr 1951
Base	Thornaby	

609 (West Riding) Sqn
Tally Ho

A/c	Vampire FB.5	Nov 1950–Jan 1951
Code	PR	1949–Apr 1951
Base	Church Fenton	

612 (County of Aberdeen) Sqn
Vigilando custodimus (We stand guard by vigilance)

A/c	Vampire FB.5	Jun 1951–Mar 1957
Code	8W	
Bases	Dyce, Leuchars and Edzell	

613 (City of Manchester) Squadron was based solely at Ringway during its post-war Royal Auxiliary Air Force existence. The first of three marks of Vampire replaced the squadron's Spitfire F.22s in March 1951 and remained until disbandment on 10 March 1957. (Via Martyn Chorlton)

613 (City of Manchester) Sqn
Semper parati (Always ready)

A/c	Vampire F.1	Feb 1951–Apr 1951
	Vampire FB.5	Feb 1951–Mar 1957
	Vampire FB.9	Jun 1954–Mar 1957
Code	Q3	1949–Apr 1951
Base	Ringway	

614 (County of Glamorgan) Sqn
Codaf I geislo (I rise to search)

A/c	Vampire F.3	Jul 1950–Dec 1951
	Vampire FB.5	Dec 51–Mar 57
	Vampire FB.9	Feb 1955–Feb 1956
Base	Llandow	

631 Sqn

A/c	Vampire F.1	Sep 1948–Feb 1949
Code	'6D'	
Base	Llanbedr	

RAF second-line units

Nos. 202, 203, 206, 208 and 210 AFS; 226, 228, 229, 233, 236 and 238 OCU; 1, 3, 4, 5, 7, 8, 9, 10 and 11 FTS; 102 and 103 FRS (Flying Refresher School); A&AEE; Air Direction Training Unit (ADTU); ATDU/AMSDU; CCGS; CFS (Central Flying School); RAF College; Central Navigation Control School/Central Air Traffic Control School; Central Gunnery School/Fighter Weapons School (CGS/FWS); CFE (inc. AFDS/Day Fighter Leaders School/Squadron); Fighter Combat School; FCCS; ECFS; EPTS (Empire Test Pilots School); Handling Squadron, RAF Manby; IAS; NGTE; RAE; Sabre

A trio of Vampire FB.5s serving with 102 FRS out of North Luffenham, which only existed from April to November 1951. WA344 has an unusual history that saw this Vampire serving in the second line initially, with 203 AFS and 102 FRS, before seeing out its days with three operational units, 98, 93 and 5 squadrons. (*Aeroplane*)

The Royal Air Force College at RAF Cranwell flew all marks of Vampire from the F.3 onwards until the mid-1960s, including this quartet of FB.9s. All four aircraft survived their service; with the exception of WX225 '8', which was SOC in November 1958, the remainder, WR264 '29', WX215 '12' and WX221 '4' were all SOC in September 1960. (*Aeroplane*)

Conversion Unit; SLAW; Station Flights – Abbotsinch, Brawdy, Culdrose, Ford, Hal Far, Lee-on-Solent, Lossiemouth, Stretton and Yeovilton; TFU/TRE; Armament Practice Station (APS) Acklington and Sylt; 26 APC Nicosia and 27 APC Butterworth; APC (MEAF); Habbaniya; Far East Examining and Training Squadron (FEES/FETS); 2, 3, 3/4, 4 and 5 Civilian Anti-Aircraft Co-Operation Unit (CAACU).

FLEET AIR ARM

700 Sqn *Experienta docet (Experience teaches)*
A/c	Sea Vampire F.20	Aug 1955 – Apr 1956
	Sea Venom FAW.21	Jan 1956 – Mar 1961
	Sea Venom FAW.20	Sep 1956 – 1959
	Sea Vampire T.22	Jul 1957 – Oct 1957
Code	FD	
Base	Ford, Yeovilton and Merryfield	

700X Sqn
A/c	Sea Vampire T.22	1957 – May 1958
Base	Ford	

702 Sqn*   *Cave ungues felis (Beware the cat's paws)*
A/c	Vampire FB.5	May 1951–May 1952
	Sea Vampire F.20	Apr 1949–Aug 1952
	Sea/Vampire T.11/22	1952
	Sea Vampire T.22	Oct 1957–Aug 1958
Code	CW or FD	
Base	Culdrose, HMS *Implacable*, HMS *Theseus*, Perseus and Lee-on-Solent	

* Redesignated 736 Squadron from August 26, 1952.

703 Sqn   *Experentia docet (Experience teaches)*
A/c	Vampire F.1	Sep 1947–Oct 1947
	Vampire F.1 (H)	1949
	Vampire FB.5	Jul 1950–Jun 1952
	Sea Vampire F.20	Oct 4198–Aug 1955
	Sea Vampire F.21	
Code	FD	
Base	Thorney Island, Lee-on-Solent and Ford	

718 Sqn
A/c	Sea Vampire T.22	Apr 1955–Dec 1955
Code	ST	
Base	Stretton and Honiley	

724 (RAN) Sqn
Learn and Live
A/c	Sea Vampire T.22	Jun 1955–1970
	Sea Venom FAW.53	Jun 1955–1973
Code	NW	
Base	Nowra	

727 Sqn   *Regere mare regite caewm (To rule the sea one must rule the sky)*
A/c	Sea Vampire T.22	Jan 1956–Dec 1960
Code	BY	
Base	Brawdy	

728 Sqn   *Descendo discimus (We learn by teaching)*
A/c	Sea Vampire F.20	Jul 1951–Mar 1955
Code	HF	
Base	Hal Far	

736 Sqn
A/c	Sea Vampire T.22	Nov 1953–Jul 1954
		Oct 1954–19Nov 58
	Sea Venom FAW.21	Oct 1957–Dec 1957
Code	LM	
Base	Lossiemouth	

738 Sqn *Parare bellum (Prepare for war)*
A/c Sea Vampire T.22 May 1954–Mar 1955
 Dec 1958–Sep 1962
 Sea Venom FAW.21 Oct 1957–Sep 1960
Code LM
Bases Brawdy and Lossiemouth

750 Sqn *Teach and strike*
A/c Sea Venom FAW.21 Jul 1960–Oct 1961
 Sea Venom FAW.22 Aug 1961–Mar 1970
 Sea Vampire T.22 Jan 1962–May 1965
Codes HF, LM and CU
Base Hal Far, Lossiemouth and Culdrose

751 Sqn
A/c Sea Venom 21 (ECM) Jun 1957–Apr 1958
Bases Lossiemouth, Brawdy, HMS *Eagle* and Hal Far

759 Sqn
A/c Vampire T.11 Jul 1952–Nov 1953
 Sea Vampire F.20 Oct 1952–Mar 1954
 Sea Vampire T.22 Nov 1953–Oct 1954
Code CW
Bases Culdrose, Lossiemouth and Milltown

764 Sqn	*Experientia expertus (Tested by trial)*	
A/c	Sea Vampire F.20	Jun 1955–Feb 1956
	Sea Vampire T.22	Jan 1955–Jun 1957
Code	FD	
Base	Ford	

766 Sqn	*Festine lente (Hasten slowly)*	
A/c	Sea Venom FAW.20	Oct 1955–Aug 1956
	Sea Vampire T.22	Jan 1956–Jul 1956
	Sea Vampire FAW.21	Aug 1956–Oct 1960
Code	VL	
Base	Yeovilton	

771 Sqn	*Non Nobis solum (Not unto us alone)*	
A/c	Vampire F.3	Jan 1951–1953
	Sea Vampire F.20	Mar 1952–Aug 1955
	Sea Vampire F.21	Jan 1951–Sep 1951
Code	FD	
Bases	Lee-on-Solent and Ford	

778 Sqn	*Ex quaestione veritas (From examination truth emerges)*	
A/c	Vampire F.1	Sep 1947–Apr 1948
	Vampire NF.10	Jul 1946
Code	FD	
Bases	Ford and Tangmere	

781 Sqn	*Reliability*	
A/c	Sea/Vampire T.11/22	Nov 1953–May 1954
	Sea Vampire T.22	Oct 1953–Dec 1964
Code	LS	
Bases	Lee-on-Solent and Ford	

787 Sqn		
A/c	Vampire F.1	Sep 1947–Feb 1950
	Vampire FB.5	Sep 1949–Aug 1953
	Sea Vampire F.20	Feb 1949–Apr 1951
	Sea Venom FAW.21	Jun 1955–Jan 1956
Bases	West Raynham and St David's	

802 Sqn	*Primus ferire (First to strike)*	
A/c	Sea Vampire T.22	Dec 1958–Jan 1959
Base	Lee-on-Solent, Lossiemouth, Brawdy and HMS *Eagle*	

805 (RAN) Sqn	*Over sea and sand*	
A/c	Sea Venom FAW.53	Mar 1958–Jun 1963
Code	M	
Bases	Nowra, HMAS *Melbourne* and Tengah	

806 Sqn	*Sursum in pugnam (Up! And into the fight)*	
A/c	Sea Vampire F.20	May 1948–Aug 1948
	Sea Vampire T.22	Apr 1958–Sep 1959
Code	LM	
Base	Eglinton, HMCS *Magnificent*, Dartmouth, Idlewild, Lossiemouth, HMS *Eagle*, Hal Far, North Front and Brawdy	

808 (RAN) Sqn	*Strength in unity*	
A/c	Sea Vampire T.22	Aug 1955–Feb 1956
	Sea Venom FAW.20	Aug 1955–Feb 1956
	Sea Venom FAW.53	Feb 1956–Dec 1958
Base	Yeovilton, HMAS *Melbourne* and Nowra	

809 Sqn	*Immortal*	
A/c	Sea Venom FAW.20	May 1954–Aug 1955
	Sea Vampire T.22	Jun 1954–Oct 1954
	Sea Venom FAW.21	May 1955–Mar 1956
		May 1956–Aug 1959
Bases	Yeovilton, HMS *Albion*, Hal Far, Merryfield, Lossiemouth, Seletar and Kai Tak	

816 (RAN) Sqn	*Imitate the action of the tiger*	
A/c	Sea Venom FAW.53	Jul 1964–Aug 1967
Code	M	
Bases	Nowra and HMAS *Melbourne*	

831 Sqn *Aquila non capit muscas (Eagles don't catch flies)*
A/c Sea Venom 21 (ECM) May 1958–Oct 1964
 Sea Vampire T.22 Nov 1958–May 1964
 Sea Venom 22 (ECM) Apr 1960–May 1966
Bases Culdrose, Watton, Abbotsinch, Lossiemouth, Sola, El Adem, Andoya, Hal Far, Hyeres, HMS *Victorious*, North Front, Valkenburg, HMS *Ark Royal*, HMS *Hermes*, Seletar, Orange, Ballykelly, Akrotiri and Rygge

890 Sqn *Caelum verrimus (We sweep the sky)*
A/c Sea Venom FAW.20 Mar 1954–May 1955
 Sea Vampire T.22 Aug 1954–May 1955
 Sea Venom FAW.21 Feb 1956–Jun 1956
Bases Yeovilton, HMS *Bulwark* and HMS *Albion*

891 Sqn *Venamur ut necemus (We search (hunt) in order that we may kill)*
A/c Sea Vampire T.22 Nov 1954–Jan 1955
 Sea Venom FAW.20 Nov 1954–Jun 1955
 Sea Venom FAW.21 Jun 1955–Apr 1956
 Sea Venom FAW.22 Dec 1957–Jul 1961
Bases Yeovilton, HMS *Ark Royal*, Hal Far, Lossiemouth, Merryfield, Brawdy, HMS *Bulwark*, North Front, Kai Tak, Khormaksar, HMS *Centaur*, Drigh Road, Bödo and Culdrose

891X Sqn
A/c Vampire FB.5 Mar 1955–Aug 1955
 Sea Vampire FAW.20 Mar 1955–Aug 1955
Base Yeovilton

892 Sqn *Strike unseen*
A/c Sea Venom FAW.21 Jul 1955–Dec 1956
 Sea Vampire T.22 Sep 1955–Feb 1956
Bases Hal Far and HMS *Eagle*

893 Sqn *Saepe feriendum (Strike often)*
A/c Sea Vampire T.22 Feb 1956–Jul 1957
 Sea Venom FAW.21 Feb 1956–Jan 1959
 Sea Venom FAW.22 Jan 1959–Feb 1960
Bases Yeovilton, HMS *Bulwark*, Ciampino, Hal Far, HMS *Eagle*, North Front, HMS *Ark Royal*, Merryfield, HMS *Victorious* and Brawdy

894 Sqn *Omnium capax ubique (Capable of anything anywhere)*
A/c Sea Venom FAW.21 Jan 1957–Mar 1957
 Sea Venom FAW.22 Jan 1957–Dec 1960
Bases Merryfield, HMS *Eagle*, Lossiemouth, Yeovilton, Hal Far, North Front, HMS *Victorious*, HMS *Albion*, Seletar and Kai Tak

Service in All Theatres

1831 Sqn *Nec temere nec timide (Neither rashly nor timidly)*
A/c Sea Vampire T.22   May 1955–Mar 1957
Code ST
Bases Hal Far, Valkenburg and Brawdy

1832 Sqn
A/c Sea Vampire T.22   Jul 1955–Mar 1957
Code CH
Bases Benson, Schleswigland and Ford

FAA second-line units
ADTU; Station Flights – Abbotsinch, Brawdy, Culdrose, Ford, Hal Far, Lee-on-Solent, Lossiemouth, Stretton and Yeovilton.

De Havilland Venom NF.3, WX796, in service with 141 Squadron at Coltishall, between June 1955 and March 1957. Only ever introduced as an interim type alongside the Meteor NF.11, the Venom NF.3 was superseded by the Javelin FAW.4, which enjoyed an even shorter service career. (Via Martyn Chorlton)

Other books you might like:

Aviation Industry Series, Vol. 5

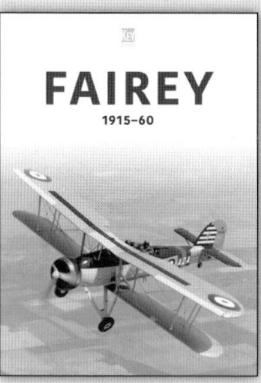

Aviation Industry Series, Vol. 1

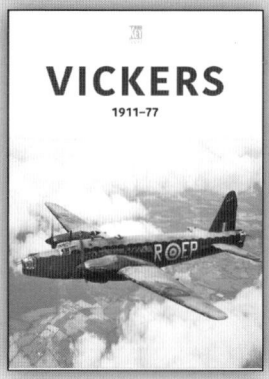

Aviation Industry Series, Vol. 4

Historic Military Aircraft Series, Vol. 22

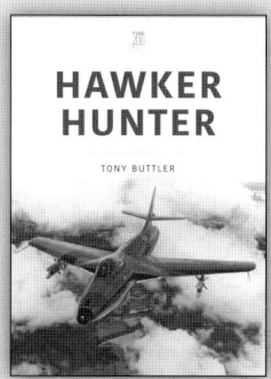

Historic Military Aircraft Series, Vol. 16

Historic Military Aircraft Series, Vol. 6

For our full range of titles please visit:
shop.keypublishing.com/books

VIP Book Club

Sign up today and receive
TWO FREE E-BOOKS

Be the first to find out about our forthcoming book releases and receive exclusive offers.

Register now at **keypublishing.com/vip-book-club**

Our VIP Book Club is a 100% spam-free zone, and we will never share your email with anyone else.
You can read our full privacy policy at: privacy.keypublishing.com